THE LITTLE BOOK ON
SELF-DISCIPLINE

GAURA NITAI DAS
MODERN MONK

The Little Book on Self-Discipline
Copyright © Gaura Nitai Das

Graphic design: Anders Grønlund
Cover: Lukas Øhlers Damgaard

ISBN: 978-87-971314-2-8.
1st edition. 1st print.

Dedicated to

… those unpolished diamonds, seeking to cultivate their true potential.

… those ambitious souls, who want to change the world starting with themselves.

… those, who do not have the self-discipline to read a big book on self-discipline.

Disclaimer

Please note that the recommendations in this book are followed at your own risk.

Content

The structure of the book

I have chosen to divide the book in three sections, which I call the elements of self-discipline. First part is knowledge, second is action and the third is the motive or the desired result. This structure is based on a bulletproof recipe for success. This is how it works.

1 The shortest distance between two points is a straight line. The first point is knowledge. Knowledge is the foundation for success and the beginning of self-discipline.

This part is therefore meant to equip you with the proper understanding of relevant principles, psychological insights and inspiration to achieve the benefits of self-discipline.

2 Knowledge without action is useless. Therefore the second part focuses on practical methods, techniques and habits, which we can use to strengthen our self-discipline, develop beneficial routines and accelerate our progress towards our respective goals in life. This is the straight line connecting the dots.

3 Third part is about motive. If we have the required knowledge and the right tools for success, what we need to do next is define our objective. What do we want from life? This part is shorter than the rest, but more philosophical. It is meant for reflection and introspection.

With self-discipline the sky is the limit, so what will you use it for? If this is clear, we can use the methods of the second part to draw a straight line between the dots, a bridge, leading from the present situation to the desired destination.

Five suggestions to get the most out of this book

1 Naturally you want maximum benefit from this book. Otherwise, why bother reading it? If that is the case, then there is a single requirement, which is more important than all other tips or techniques put together.

You have to be motivated! You need to be driven by a desire to learn and to grow. If you are, then I am certain that you will find valuable information on every page, which you can use in life, experiment with and achieve amazing results.

If you don't have a strong desire for developing self-discipline, it may be because the word 'discipline' doesn't come across as sexy per se. You may be thinking of uniformed students or something like that. That's why I have spent the first chapter glorifying the benefits of self-discipline to guarantee that your excitement is aroused from the very beginning.

2 Food for thought is great, but over-eating is not. Books like this are meant for more than entertainment and killing time. Please consider which ideas are most relevant for you to implement in your life. This is especially relevant, when you read the second part of the book, which is packed with suggestions, experiments and habits you can play with. So after each reading, please consider what you have read, and how you can use it in your situation.

3 Read with a pen and a marker. I would be absolutely flattered if you make your copy more personal by adding your own notes. Underline if you find a suggestion you can use. That makes the important points easier to find later on, if you decide to re-read it. Then you will be able to quickly go through it in the future, and remind yourself of the essence of each chapter.

4 Have a notebook, reserved for the topic of self-discipline, closeby when you are reading. Taking notes fortifies remembrance. You might keep a diary for noting your observations as you experiment. What did you do, and how did it work? It is interesting to look back at your experiences and remind yourself of the lessons learned.

5 Come back to it every now and then. Don't try to implement the methods all at once. For the most part it will just be an unnecessary overload. Better to read one chapter at a time and note what inspires you. If you just pick up one good habit at a time, you can focus on solidifying it and come back for more later on. This little book is very patient, and will happily stay on your shelf waiting for you.

Introduction

Why this little book?

A couple of years ago I was invited to a high school to speak about eastern philosophy. The students were listening attentively, even though the topic may have been foreign to them. After the presentation I opened up for questions, and they started inquiring about my life as a monk. Then, as I passionately started speaking about self-discipline and the value thereof, I could feel their focus intensify. Here was something they could really use! That made me reflect upon my own time in high school.

If I could give my former self a gift, it would be my love of self-discipline! Unfortunately I can't. But maybe I can give it to you. I have tried to put that love on paper in these pages. Self-discipline is a wonderful tool, which can be used by anyone in any aspect of life. It is the key to all self-development. With it, one can open the doors to one's dreams, achieve one's goals and – most importantly – raising the quality of life.

Those who need self-discipline the most are, however, also those who have the hardest time pulling themselves together to work on it – not to mention reading a book! That is why this is not a grand, in-depth study, but a short and concise, easy-to-read manual, which is practically applicable. A book that I wish someone would have gifted me as a youth. Well, maybe in the next life.

In the Danish language, in which I originally wrote the manuscript, there is no little book on the subject. The availability of books in English is larger, and there is more to choose from, so my initial thought was sticking to the Danish audience. However, after continuous requests for an English translation, I decided to surrender. So here you go. It can be read by anyone, but is especially written with the youth in mind.

Why the youth? Because it's not easy growing up in the modern world! Life is like a minefield of distractions, temptations and pitfalls. Without self-discipline, you are a sitting duck in a war zone. But if you have it, you're bulletproof.

Who am I to teach you about self-discipline?

Good question, and if you had asked my parents, high school teachers or old friends the same question a couple of years ago, they would have fallen off their chairs laughing.
I was living in my parents' basement, rolling joints and dreaming of a better world. An idealist, but as lazy as they come. I had plenty of time to study conspiracy theories, but never enough to do my homework. I somehow made it through high school without getting expelled. My father used to say I work best under pressure. But the truth is I only worked under pressure!

When I graduated from high school I was bewildered, to say the least, about which path to choose. So rather than moving straight on to further education, I decided to buy myself some time by signing up for military service. I soon came to regret that, all too late. It turned out for the better, however. I got some good habits in the military and my fascination for self-discipline slowly awakened.

After the military, I became a lot more responsible. I had

a job and a girlfriend. I became a vegetarian. I started experimenting with meditation and began reading a lot of books. And then one day I met a monk. I never expected to meet a monk in the middle of Copenhagen. We had an interesting talk and his wisdom and calm happiness turned on something inside of me. He invited me to the local temple. I didn't know there was a local temple, but I agreed to come over, encouraged by the vegetarian feast he spoke about.

They say it takes seven seconds to get a first impression. The first seven seconds in the temple blew me away. It was unforgettable. And as a result I have now been living and studying as a monk for the past six years. My studies centre on meditation, philosophy and psychology.

We work for self-purification, believing that the highest form of happiness arises naturally when we are in a state of mind free of lust, anger and greed, and live our lives as a selfless sacrifice in the service of others.

I have chosen to live a life with a level of self-discipline that makes my time in the military seem like playtime in kindergarten. Let me mention a few of the principles we live by: we get up before four in the morning, and start our day with prayers of gratitude and group meditation. Then we have private meditation for two hours, working on self-purification and mental control. We are celibate, and avoid intoxication, gambling and meat. The question may come up: so, how do you have fun? The thing is, if you can enter into a state of serene internal satisfaction, you need not look for satisfaction externally.

Some may look upon our lifestyle as torture, but I don't experience it like that. In fact I love it. I am grateful to the monk that showed me the path. I feel a deep sense of purpose and meaning. My relationships are much richer, I feel vibrant with good health, and I have been given tools – like self-discipline – to accomplish what I would have previously considered impossible.

I owe a lot to my many mentors, who are helping me on my path to becoming the person that I want to be, and have inspired my pursuit of self-discipline. I am not yet where I want to be, but the journey has just begun and compared to before it is a breath-taking one.

My inspiration

Since leaving the military I have been obsessed with self-development. I have read the works of many western authors from philosophers to self-help coaches, psychologists, neurologists, philanthropists, motivational speakers and so on. I have learned a lot from modern people, but the wisdom of the East has captured my heart.

My main inspiration is the crown jewel of Eastern philosophy – the Bhagavad-gita – and those who adhere to its teachings. Bhagavad-gita is part of the Vedas, the ancient scriptures containing the timeless philosophy of old India, written in the Sanskrit language more than 5,000 years ago. Despite their antiquity, the lessons they contain are as relevant today as ever, as is evidenced by many of the principles being echoed throughout history and finding their way into many of the popular self-help books of today.

This little book is an attempt at taking the essence of that timeless wisdom and the crème de la crème of modern self-help, bringing together the best advice on self-discipline from two worlds of thought, in a bite-size publication, for the progressive elevation of the modern reader. Enjoy!

1. PART

KNOWLEDGE

"An investment in knowledge pays the best interest"
- Benjamin Franklin

Following the teachings of the Vedas, I have chosen to divide self-discipline in three elements: knowledge, action and motive, which in Sanskrit is called sambandha, abhideya and prayojana. These three elements have an amazing interplay.

How so? When the cornerstone of knowledge has been laid, we have a good starting point. We are equipped with the necessary information of relevant factors, which we ought to know in the process of self-discipline, and how they interact with each other.

Knowledge implies knowledge of both action and motive. "What is your desired goal, and how do you get there?" When you have the required knowledge, and you have an inspiring goal, a motive for action, then all you need is to act on that knowledge to reach your goal.

Part one of the book is knowledge. That is placing our cornerstone. To define discipline and self-discipline and account for the difference between the two is a good place to start. The advantages of having a strong self-discipline and the disadvantages of not having it will also be touched upon. I will also go through how self-discipline can theoretically be strengthened, and discuss the obstacles we will meet on the way toward it.

CHAPTER 1

The freedom of choice

"Through self-discipline comes freedom"
– Aristoteles, Greek philosopher

I wake up before the alarm rings. It's 1:47 in the dead of night. I could go back to sleep. Should I? It's a Sunday, which for most people translates to lying in bed throughout the morning.

The silence of night is broken by laughter. Noisy youths are making their way back home from a night out. I used to be just like them - young, wild and "free". I decide to jump-start the day, rising from my bed, which is actually just a thin yoga mat, and begin my morning routine with a verse from the Bhaga-vad-gita quietly echoing in my mind: "What is night for all beings, is the time of awakening for the self-controlled. And what is the time of awakening for all beings is night for the introspective." There are many points to be understood from this verse, but at this moment, the literal meaning is quite fitting.

The key to freedom

I grew up thinking freedom is doing what I wanted to do, when I wanted to do it. If I would like to sleep, then I would be *free* to sleep. If I wanted to smoke, then I would be *free* to smoke. Following my impulses, whatever that entailed, was just an exhibition of freedom. I often ask people: "what does freedom mean to you?". And that is often the answer I get: doing what you want to do. But is that really freedom?

You may want to stay in bed, but can you overcome that initial urge to hit the snooze and roll over? You may want to follow a diet, but can you control yourself when the sweets are being passed around? You may want to stay home and work on an important assignment, but can you resist the temptation, when your friends call and ask you out? Please don't get me wrong. I am not saying you have to torture yourself and reject all the fun and exciting things in life. What I am saying is that freedom is determined by our ability to make conscious choices. In the ancient *Bhagavad-gita*, written 5.000 years ago, there is mention of 'regulative principles of freedom'. Regulation and freedom seem to be opposing forces. But are they really?

In Sanskrit, the word for self-discipline is *tapasya*, which literally translates as 'to shine'. It was common for the ancient *yogis*, to undergo all sorts of voluntary hardships, like submerging oneself in ice-cold rivers running through the Himalayan Mountains, or going to the forests to meditate with vows of silence, surviving on roots and berries. Crazy stuff! But "why?", one may ask. For developing self-discipline, achieving control of the mind, and the consequent freedom of being able to choose.

Freedom is having a choice, and self-discipline enables you to make a good one, because you are not forced to act on your immediate desires. It also allows you to more readily transgress the comfort-zone, and do things, which you are not necessarily inspired to, but which will give good results. If we think about it, there are quite a lot of things, that are initially tough, difficult, or maybe just boring, but that will give good long-term results. Working out for example is hard and painful, but if you want to be fit and healthy it is necessary. Studying may at times be tiresome and uninspiring, but if you want to have the career of your dreams that is a sacrifice you must make. Saving money for the future while you're working so you can retire early or spend a year travelling the world might be a good idea, but then you have to be able to undergo some voluntary austerities and cut down on your expenses. If we boil down self-discipline to its concentrated essence, it consists of two parts. 1) Being able to do what you don't want to do. 2) Being able to not do what you want to do.

That our success and freedom in life to a large degree depend on what seems to restrict our freedom may be an inconvenient truth. But it doesn't mean life has to be a walk through the desert. But it does mean that you have to be able to delay gratification, and wait for a bigger and better result. At this point, I would like to share with you two amazing verses from the *Bhagavad-gita*: "That which in the beginning may be bitter like poison, but sweet as nectar in the end is a higher happiness, than that which is initially sweet but ends up being bitter." If that didn't blow your mind the first time, read it again. So with self-discipline we can delay the sensation of pleasure, patiently waiting for something far superior.

You want one now or two later?

In the 1970's the renowned psychologist Walter Mischel began one of the most elaborate studies of self-discipline and human behaviour. His methods were simple. He would use children of various ages as subjects and test their level of self-discipline by placing before them a marshmallow, a cookie or a treat of their liking. It would then be explained to the children, that they were free to eat it now if they wanted.

But if they were able to abstain for twenty-five minutes the stakes would be raised, and they would be rewarded with two sweets instead of one.

Dr. Mischel has conducted thousands of such experiments under various conditions, and his discoveries are fascinating. Some are simple truths; others are technical explanations of human behaviour, venturing into complex neuroscience. But the most noteworthy discovery is that children who exhibit a high level of self-control generally grow up to become significantly more successful. Following his subjects years down the line, he found that those who had passed the marshmallow test were healthier, happier, had better incomes, lower divorce rates, etc. This strongly indicates the tremendous benefit of self-discipline on an acknowledged scientific foundation.

The path to greatness

The primary benefit of self-discipline is the freedom of choice, and that opens the door to innumerable additional benefits. Thus self-discipline is a transformative characteristic, with an unlimited potential. Time and time again it has transformed beginners into world champions, ideas into ingenious inventions, and dreams into living reality. It is with self-discipline, that a young student, mindful of the future, chooses to study while the classmates are partying. It was with self-discipline that Thomas Edison stubbornly kept working on the light bulb despite 10.000 failed attempts. It was with self-discipline that Michael Jordan, although initially rejected from his high school basketball team, became one of the greatest athletes of all times.

Greatness is never a coincidence: it is always a result of a continuous, determined effort. But, someone may object, it seems certain people are just born more privileged. Even if someone has been born incredibly gifted, they still have to develop their gifts, if they don't want to squander them on mediocre achievements. Nothing extraordinary comes about without self-discipline. But with self-discipline, almost anything is possible.

A prerequisite for love

Love is probably not the first thing that comes to mind when we talk about self-discipline. But think about it. Is it possible to love without self-discipline? Can we talk about love, if one is not able to move beyond one's personal needs and put those of the beloved first? It may be that love came first, but the result is self-discipline and a corresponding behaviour.

It is with love that a mother decides to put aside her own needs for the sake of her child. It is with love that a couple can stay loyal to each other and stick together despite challenges. It is with love that one can dedicate oneself to a higher cause. But without self-discipline love is insufficient, and the conscious choice of loving may change according to circumstances. Self-discipline is freedom, and love is being able to surrender that freedom to another person or a higher cause.

Whatever one may want from life - be it success, wealth, love or the entire package - one has to work for it, and for that, self-discipline is a necessity. It is, as Abraham Lincoln once said: "Things may come to those who wait, but only the things left by those who hustle."

SHORT SUMMARY

More self-discipline means more freedom

*The ability to delay gratification
makes one prosperous*

The surrender freedom is true love

CHAPTER 2

From no-discipline, to discipline to self-discipline

"The only discipline that lasts is self-discipline"
- Bum Phillips, american football coach

What if I don't have it?

Would you have been able to pass the marshmallow test as a child? Personally, I am doubtful how my mischievous former self would have handled the challenge. When you ask my parents about my childhood, self-discipline is probably the last characteristic they would describe me with. And if self-discipline doesn't seem to come natural, is there then any hope for a prosperous future, or is someone predestined because they picked the short straw in the genetic lottery to become a loser, a social outcast, or maybe even, God forbid, a celibate monk?

Not necessarily. It's not so much the cards that you've been dealt. It's more important how you play your hand. It is confirmed by neuroscience that we can actually reshape the structure of our brains by our thoughts and actions, and train the specific areas relevant to self-discipline such as the frontal lobes that deals with choice. Even for those who accept the infallible law of karma, the Vedas explain that human beings have been given free will, and with that we can change our thoughts, environment, actions and hence our destiny. At the risk of turning overly autobiographical, I will share with you my personal experience of moving from no-discipline, to discipline and towards self-discipline.

Under the sway of the mind

I used to smoke a bit too much cannabis in high school. It had been going on for years before my parents realized it, but when they did, they naturally started worrying about me. I thought they were just being hysterical. "Don't worry, mom. Dad, everything is under control. I can quit if I want to, no problem." I believed it myself, and just to prove a point I vowed not to smoke for a month. "That shouldn't be a problem. Right?" And it wasn't. At least not until a few days later when I found myself on my bike heading for Freetown Christiania's Pusher Street.

It was an internal tug-of-war, a fight for supremacy. I felt like the forces of right and wrong were competing, and that their battlefield was the inside of my head. You've probably seen Donald Duck depicted with an angel on one shoulder and a devil on the other. It was something like that. I later came to know these as the mind and the intelligence. The intelligence pleaded: "You promised not to smoke! You said, that you could stop if you wanted to! Come on. It hasn't even been a week!" In the other corner, the mind was making its case: "What a stupid vow! Chill out, the weather is so nice! You need to relax."

I was dragged back and forth through the streets of Copenhagen. I changed my mind, and with that my direction, several times under the pathetic sway of fleeting emotions. Eventually I relented, my determination caved in. I had to swallow my words and with that my pride, and admit to myself that I didn't have the self-discipline to stick with my decision.

Receiving the seed of discipline

According to the dictionary, discipline is defined as controlling behaviour with a system of consequential reward and punishment. If you don't behave, you will be punished, and if you act nicely, you will be rewarded. That is discipline. It works, as long as it is enforced. That's why our parents used it on us, why it's happening every day in the classrooms, and why the police use it to enforce law and order in society. But since the word discipline is often associated with punishment and strictness, rebellious youths are often averse to it.

But sometimes, externally enforced discipline is a necessity, and can be a stepping-stone to a higher mode of life. It can help one become responsible and stay out of trouble. Maybe it would have made a difference, if there had been some obvious consequences for breaking my vow to my parents, or some expectancy of a reward for following through with it.

Nobody likes to be disciplined, but it can be a tremendous help. At least I had that experience during military service. It was good for me having to wake up early in the morning, take orders and do as I was told. Why? It helped me overrule the dictates of the mind, at least for as long as I was under supervision. I didn't feel like ironing my shirts, keeping order in my locker or polishing my boots, not to mention doing drills, walking long distances in the rain through muddy fields or having sergeants constantly correcting me. I hated it, but I am grateful I had that experience, because from that seed of discipline, self-discipline got a chance to sprout.

Self-discipline

Receiving the seed of discipline is only the beginning. Seeds need water to sprout, and then they need sunlight and nutrition to grow. Eventually, after many years a tree will grow luxuriantly and start providing fruits in abundance. Similarly, the seed of discipline should be received and cultivated carefully: only after enduring the process of cultivation will one get to taste the sweet result of self-discipline.

To act under discipline is to depend on an external authority. But those who are self-disciplined no longer require any authority to watch over them and swing the whip to get stuff done. Such persons are motivated, enthusiastic and self-propelled. Willing to work hard to reach their goals, also when they are alone and nobody is watching.

Now I am living as a monk in a temple, and as opposed to my time in the military, this is a conscious choice that I made, because I want a certain result and I have faith in the process. I am not forced to wake up at 2.00 in the night. No one tells me to take a cold shower in the morning, and my mother would love nothing more than for me to re-enter society and find a girlfriend. So why am I doing all this? I am cultivating the seed. I am learning to deal with my mind, and take control over it to experience the freedom of choice. I am not trying to advertise myself as superior in any way. I am just giving this as an example, to illustrate that it is possible to move from no-discipline, to discipline, to self-discipline.

Why even bother?

I want you to imagine a scenario. Think of a chariot with five horses. You are the passenger and decide the destination. But if the charioteer doesn't have control of the horses, you might be heading for danger, or maybe you're going nowhere, depending of course on the impulses of the horses. Same thing happens when intelligence doesn't control the senses. This is equivalent to having no discipline. We have five senses, which are attracted to different objects. If we don't keep them under control, they will drag us around senselessly. As such, being undisciplined is an awkward and unreliable state of existence.

Discipline may be better, because at least there is some control; it is depending of course on who has that control. If you have been disciplined by the al-Qaeda, then it would probably have been better to remain undisciplined. But if you are a disciple acting under the instruction of an enlightened spiritual master, then that is a blessing for the whole world. The value of discipline finally depends on who is holding the reins.

The best is to strive for self-discipline, and taking personal responsibility for one's progress in life. That necessitates controlling the mind and the senses, which is an awesome challenge. It is also admitted in the Bhagavad-gita, that this is extremely difficult. "The senses are so strong, that they may forcibly carry away the mind even of a man of discrimination who is endeavouring to control them." But simultaneously, the value of self-discipline is stressed. "One who can withdraw his senses from sense objects, as the tortoise draws its limbs within a shell, is fixed in perfect consciousness." Such a person can choose. Again, that is freedom.

SHORT SUMMARY

Discipline is doing what you're told

Self-discipline is taking responsibility and mastering one's choices

Discipline is a stepping-stone to self-discipline

CHAPTER 3

The mind of a disciple

"We all carry seeds of greatness within us, but we need an image as a point of focus in order that they may sprout."
- Epictetus, stoic philosopher.

The word disciple comes from the Latin "discipulus" and means "the learner". Traditionally, a disciple had a master or a guru, from whom one receives knowledge and training. That has worked out well for millennia, and so the education of today rests on the same principle of teachers and students. The principle is the still the same, but the details may vary. So considering ourselves modern disciples, or learners, how do we find the right teacher today? What is the state of mind to be cultivated and how can we accelerate the learning process and sustain it for a lifetime?

The shortcut is a person

It is essential to have teachers who can introduce us to the world and its concepts and get us started on our journey. Without them we are nowhere. Albert Einstein once said, "We owe a lot to the Indians, who taught us how to count, without which no worthwhile scientific discovery could have been made." Just consider that the one of the greatest mathematicians and physicists in history was thanking our ancestors for paving the way for his science by providing us basic counting. In that sense, he was humble. He acknowledged their contribution. Another great scientist Isaac Newton similarly confessed: "If I have seen further, it is by standing on the shoulders of Giants."

Please consider how much of our knowledge, ability and character is self-manifest. Practically none of it! Knowledge, ability and character eternally exist as principles, and we may have the good fortune of coming in contact with it through our teachers. So whatever one is looking for is already out there, and someone has found it.

There was no need for Albert Einstein to reinvent the counting system, nor is there a need for anyone to reinvent the wheel. It is already there as it works. One simply has to connect with the carriers of the knowledge, ability and character one may desire and receive it from them. In the Bhagavad-gita it is advised: "Just try to learn the truth by approaching a spiritual master, inquire from him and render service. The self-realised souls can reveal knowledge unto you because they have seen the truth."

The search for a teacher

In ancient India it was custom that an aspiring disciple would search for master. If the master saw the candidate fit, he would then accept him as a student. Our contemporary situation is little different. In most cases we don't select our teachers. They are given to us. The teaching profession is not very profitable nowadays. Teachers are often disrespected, and as such, it has become a less desirable occupation. Since the standard has therefore been lowered, one cannot expect that the teachers given to us will be of the highest calibre.

Since a good mentor is so crucial to our personal development, why should one remain satisfied with those that were assigned by the educational system? Why not take responsibility for one's progress in life, and seek out an inspiring role model one can take guidance from?

The statement that "when the student is ready, the teacher shall appear" often holds true. So in the search for a teacher, the first requirement is having a strong desire to find one. Secondly, one has to be able to see the opportunities as they arise and not shy away from them. Teachers are kind, generally, and most take pleasure in sharing what they have learned. So as the Bible saying goes: "Ask and it will be given to you; seek and ye shall find". Don't ask, and you will probably not receive anything. But if one finds a qualified teacher, and approaches them with humility and an honest desire to learn, one will likely be surprised by that good fortune may arise.

But really it is not needed to be in close physical proximity of a great mentor to gain great value from them, though it's highly recommendable to get that close association. The best teachers, mentors and masters are patiently waiting on the bookshelves of the world. Reading gives you the wonderful opportunity of intimate one-on-one time with the most highly esteemed mentors that have ever been. Especially today there is no excuse not to seek further education. Books are cheaper than ever before. Knowledge on every topic is available in the easily digestible formats of videos, podcasts and audio files.

A foundation of respect

So what should be the attitude of a disciple? How does one relate to one's teachers in such a way as to derive the highest benefit? In our bodies we need strong connective tissues, tendons and ligaments for the bones and muscles to cooperate nicely. Those ligaments and tissues are the relationship between the student and the teacher, which makes the learning process effective and pleasant. That relationship is based on respect. If the student doesn't understand his position in relation to the teacher, or the teacher is not a sincere well-wisher of the student, the transaction of knowledge and skill is obstructed. But if the relationship is good, the result is more likely to be fruitful.

Some teachers are inspiring, skilful and knowledgeable and naturally generate an atmosphere of respect. Others are boring, incompetent and demoralising. One may ask: "Should one be humble and respectful towards a person, who has not earned our respect?" When I talk about respect in education, I am not necessarily talking about awe and reverence, but appreciation and gratitude. If one has difficulties respecting the teacher, try to look beyond the person, and respect him or her as a representative of the subject matter, and respect that.

The thing is, if one has a good attitude, listens attentively and tries to do one's best while communicating respectm then one's teacher will feel appreciated. That may very well be the needed inspiration for the teacher to rise to the occasion and give his or her best. If they don't, nothing is lost. At least one got the chance to practice the universally valued behaviour of being respectful. An atmosphere of respect makes good teachers great, and can motivate the unmotivated to make a more wholehearted effort.

In Vedic culture this respect is practised to an extreme degree. In fact, it is recommended that one sees one's teacher as a direct representative of God, and consequently respect the teacher as one would respect God personified. The principle is respect, and the detail may vary in terms of time, place and circumstance. With respect, however, you can create an atmosphere in which your teachers feel inspired to invest in you as person, not because they are paid for it, but because they genuinely wish for you the best!

Remaining an eternal student

There's a lovely tale in Vedic literature that conveys an amazing lesson. Once, a king had a son, and the king was very insistent that his son begin his education as soon possible. The son was still just a newborn, and the king was told, "It's too early. Let him enjoy his childhood for some time." The king decided to consult his minister, who advised him, "The best situation for your son's education is found in between the breasts of women." The king was visibly puzzled by the answer, but before he could formulate a reply, the minister starts laughing, "The best time for your son's education starts the moment he loses attraction for his mother's breasts, and stops when he starts noticing the breasts of the young girls."

The point is to not get distracted. The golden years in between breast sucking and breast seeking are in most cases relatively short, but can be lengthened indefinitely with the aid of self-discipline. It applies both ways, not only to boys. One who can remain focused despite temptations and distractions can remain fixed on the path of the eternal student. The Bhagavad-gita confirms, "Therefore, in the very beginning, curb this great symbol of distraction, lust, by controlling the senses and slay this destroyer of knowledge and self-realisation."

Ego is the enemy

Besides lust the greatest distraction for the progressive disciple is probably ego. Actually, ego just means identity, and there is nothing wrong with that. So when we talk about ego in a negative context, we are referring to the false ego or a distorted perception of oneself. This inaccurate self-image becomes an obstacle when one encounters some initial success and because of that, starts thinking of oneself as perfect or good enough, and thus there is no incentive for further development.

A modern example of someone who remained a humble student despite of success is Kirk Hammett, a young guitarist who was invited to join the metal group Metallica. For others, such an honour may have carried them away, but not Kirk. He was humbled by the opportunity, so much so that he started searching for a teacher, despite the fact that he was already a professional musician playing for one of the most popular groups at that time. He knew there was still so much more for him to learn, so he found a legendary guitarist, Joe Satriani and enrolled as his student. He took corrections, did homework and practised persistently.

Imagine the power and potential of having such an attitude. How quickly do we become complacent and proud of what we know? Too soon. Because there will never be a time, when one has learned it all. In the Bhagavad-gita there is a list of the symptoms of true knowledge. It is noteworthy that the first item is mentioned is humility, and the second is pridelessness. But wait, that seems a little repetitive. Aren't they synonymous? Yes, indeed.

SHORT SUMMARY

Everyone needs a teacher

Respect and humility accelerate learning

Always remain a student

CHAPTER 4

Modern challenges

"O learned one, in this Iron Age of Kali men almost always have but short lives. They are quarrelsome, lazy, misguided, unlucky and, above all, always disturbed."
- A Vedic prophecy recorded in the Srimad-Bhagavtam

Technology, entertainment and social media

The modern world is in many ways very different from the world that our parents, grandparents and former generations grew up in. New technology has brought about new opportunities. Today you can spend your time in many more meaningless ways than ever before. Previously, it wasn't even an option to waste your life on computer games or Netflix, but now with the push of a button you can summon innumerable varieties of entertainment, information and distractions both day and night. So, is that good or bad?

As Shakespeare said, "Things are neither good nor bad, but our thinking makes them so." The value of something is always dependent on how it is used. It is good to use a knife to slice bread. It is not so good to cut your forearm or stab people. Technology, entertainment and social media can be enlightening and informative, but they can also be black holes of irresistible force, which consume the intelligence, creativity and the very life force of the next generation.

Where is the impetus to do something exciting with your

life, when you can just put on a movie, and get all the excitement you need without lifting a finger? It is also easier to build a character in a computer game than real life. Why make an extra endeavour to show genuine appreciation of people when you can just like their Facebook-status?

Temptations, intoxications and stimulants

Modern people are the guinea pigs of a new type of psychological stimuli. We have to deal with smartphones that are constantly vibrating. Our senses are under constant bombardment of millions of sounds and images, designed to capture our attention and convince us to spend money on things we don't need.

Everyone knows that alcohol kills brain cells, yet how many would object to the youth celebrating life, partying and drinking a few times a week? In many parts of the world that is the standard nowadays. But just because it is normal, does that mean it is harmless? Even if you don't go wild on weekends, you've probably eaten more sugar by the age of three, than people used to eat during a lifetime one hundred years ago.

It would be naïve to think that these things do not cause scars, deep impressions and disruptions in our consciousness in ways that previous generations would not have been able to fathom in their wildest imagination. How do these modern influences affect our concentration, memory and sense of self-discipline?

I am grateful that I encountered positive influences early in life that helped me change my ways, quit intoxicants and be more cautious about modern stimuli. But I cannot help but regret how much potential ran down the drain during those wild years of mine, and how much potential is still being squandered by many youths the world over.

Stress, depression and anxiety

Another widespread phenomenon of the modern world is mental illness. The most prominent forms of which are stress, anxiety and depression. To contemplate how ordinary these conditions have become is alarming.

For example, a study of Danish university students revealed that 45% are showing symptoms of stress on a daily basis, and during examination periods the number is significantly greater. Many are caving in under pressure due to high expectations, and take sick leave due to depression and stress.

It is interesting to compare this tendency to Vedic society wherein the first qualification of the intellectuals is just being calm and peaceful. If the intellectuals of the future are literally falling apart, where does that lead us?

It has now become common to rely on antidepressants and happy pills just to get through the day. In fact, every tenth Dane has been prescribed antidepressants. A quick search on Google for social anxiety will give you hits of astounding numbers on the rise.

A vaccine of self-discipline

Is it possible that with the help of self-discipline one could acquire behavioural traits that could protect one from these modern challenges, in the same way that a vaccine immunizes one to a disease?

Without either discipline or self-discipline it is impossible to develop skills, talents and character. Those years when my self-discipline was at its lowest were also the years that I least experienced development. The more I slacked, the stronger my bad habits grew, and not having self-control affected my self-esteem, not toward a strong sense of healthy humility, but toward anxiety and depression.

These modern challenges reinforce one another. If for example one is suffering from social anxiety, it is convenient to be able to disappear into parallel universes of series and computer games, so you don't have to deal with people in the real world. If one sits in front of a screen for most of the day, one will be bereft of the physical and emotional stimulus that we need. This can easily result in depression, which one can then try to escape by drinking or hiding in a cloud of hash smoke.

You don't have to stick to the stereotypes. The modern world offers a broad variety of alternatives, so there is plenty of scope for be original and ruin one's life in a unique and distinct way.

Self-discipline is more important than ever before. We require it to protect our sanity, dreams and ambitions against the many distractions, temptations and pitfalls that threaten us at every step. The vaccine of self-discipline doesn't carry any negative side effects. It is like a magic potion.

SHORT SUMMARY

More distractions than ever before

Don't become victimized by the culture

Protect your dreams with self-discipline

CHAPTER 5

Your best friend or worst enemy

"For him who has conquered the mind, the mind is the best of friends, but for one who has failed to do so, the mind will remain the greatest enemy."
– Bhagavad-gita

Have you ever done something, that you knew was wrong? Something that you didn't want to do, but you just couldn't control yourself and you immediately felt a sense of regret? What is that force, pushing us to act against our own self-interest?

The senses, mind and the intelligence

Our senses are constantly receiving impressions: forms, colours, sound, smell, taste and touch. The mind categorizes them as good or bad based on previous experience. Two individuals can therefore have very different experiences of the same thing. If for example you were deeply traumatized as a child after being attacked by a dog, you will most likely think differently about dogs compared to a person whose best friend in childhood was the family dog.

When the mind has judged an impression as good or bad, the intelligence then decides how to respond. The more intelligence, the more possibilities. If for example a small child sees a dog, and the mind categorizes the dog as being good, the child will naturally be excited, but without experience, not knowing what to do with that excitement. A more experienced person will have more options. He knows that dogs likes being scratched behind the ear, on the belly and catch sticks flying in mid-air.

So the mind is putting labels on objects and the intelligence decides what to do with them. But both the mind's perceptions and labelling on the world around us, as well as our reaction to it happen mostly on autopilot without us being aware of the process. If you see a delicious piece of cake, you don't decide to be attracted or not. It just happens.

Are you your own worst enemy?

Every day we choose things which are not in our self-interest. Every time we eat that greasy junk that we will regret later. Every time we foolishly waste our hard-earned money on things that we don't need. Every time we postpone an important task that we will eventually have to face, we are acting against our own self-interest. Why are we doing that? Isn't life difficult enough already?

An enemy can be defined as an entity, which is acting to the detriment of one's well-being. It is therefore in no way an exaggeration to claim that we are often our own worst enemies. That should sound the alarm! Let us stop fighting ourselves. Let us stop making choices that are injurious to our potential future selves and our dreams! Let us no longer be our own worst enemy. Let us rather form an alliance with the mind, and become our own best friend and well-wisher. That is not to say you should become an egotistical, navel-gazing narcissist. But it is difficult to add value to the lives of others without dealing with your own mind first.

Become your own best friend

The mind is a friend when it is under the control of good intelligence. The mind can be compared to a child, which needs a helping hand. Therefore it is important that the intelligence can be a responsible parent, helping to identify things correctly, so they can make good decisions together.

Children often don't know what is best for them, and neither does the mind. It just acts on impulse. Therefore it must be trained and educated. It shouldn't be allowed to act loosely without supervision of the intelligence. This is very much a question about awareness.

Raising a child is hard work. It is easier to spoil than to discipline, but an experienced and loving parent knows that they will need to enforce discipline with the child's future in mind, and that is an expression of love. So try not to think of self-discipline as a sort of self-inflicted punishment, but as the very essence of self-love and care.

Next time you are about to do something, which you know is not a good idea, you can tell yourself: "Don't do it!", "Stop!", "I forbid you to eat that pizza!" How about trying in a more compassionate tone? Try this: "I know that you want to eat that pizza. But I also know how you are going to feel afterwards, and I love you too much to let you go through that." "I know that you don't want to study for your final exam, but I also know how bad you are going to feel if you flunk it. And I love you too much to allow that." "I know you want to stay in bed all day, but I also know how much you want (insert your dream here), and staying in bed is just not going to get you there!"

You might be able to control your mind with sheer force. But the ropes of love are much stronger, and once the mind has been disciplined, it is only the laws of nature and your own priorities, which are deciding what you can and what you cannot do with your life.

SHORT SUMMARY

*The mind works by a pattern
that can be changed*

*Stop allowing actions detrimental
to your growth*

Self-discipline is parenting the mind with love

CHAPTER 6

Pleasure and satisfaction

"It is the nature of the wise to resist pleasures, but the foolish to be a slave to them."
– Epictetus, Greek philosopher

Sense pleasure

Except for those who possess humour and see ghosts, most of us have just five senses: sight, hearing, taste, touch and smell. The primary function of the senses is to help us interact with the world around us and collect knowledge about our surroundings. Without the senses we would be helpless. They are a great asset, but just like the mind, they need to be controlled.

Why must they be controlled? Because they have a secondary function: pleasure, which tends to spin out of control. When the five senses come in contact with the world around us we experience form, sound, taste, touch and aroma. This sensual stimulation is interpreted by the mind as good or bad, and based on our previous experiences we are attracted to and repulsed by different objects.

The problem is that our interpretation of good and bad often is treacherous! A mouse picks up the smell of cheese and its mouth starts running with saliva. It equates cheese with sense pleasure and blinded by lust, it runs toward its own destruction, not noticing the trap. In a similar way, we often fall victim of illusion expecting to find happiness at the end of pleasure.

There is a profound verse in the Bhagavad-gita explaining the pursuit of pleasure as the fountainhead of frustration and dissatisfaction. Why? Because it is temporary. Think about it. You are eating a good box of chocolate and that is enjoyable, no doubt. But even before finishing your mind begins to lament. "Oh no! It will soon be over!" To consider pleasure the basis of our happiness forces us to restlessly move from one sense stimulation to the next in the pursuit of short termed gratification. Therefore, the Bhagavad-gita concludes: "He who is not disturbed by the incessant flow of desires, can find peace, and not he who seeks to satisfy such desires."

The point is not that it is forbidden to enjoy the senses. But if sense pleasure is the foundation of your happiness, you are setting yourself of for disappointment. It is obviously short-sighted. Something like living on a diet of pizza and coke. Luckily, there is an alternative.

Satisfaction

Pleasure comes from the outside, satisfaction comes from the inside. They are diametrical opposites. Think about it: How can you be satisfied and eager for pleasure simultaneously? Then you are obviously not satisfied. If you were, why would you be eager for pleasure? The more satisfied you are, the more the need for pleasure will subside, and dwindle into insignificance.

A good example is being horny. In Danish the word for horny is "liderlig", which actually means to be suffering. Isn't that precisely what sexual impulse is: a state of itchy dissatisfaction we feverishly try to mitigate? If the goal is temporary enjoyment, sex is the undisputed king of pleasure. But if the goal is satisfaction, sex is no more a solution than a scratch to an itch.

Scratching the surface is merely dealing with the symptom, and is will most likely just aggravate the condition. It would be wiser to find out the root cause of the problem, and deal with that. So if we want to solve our problem of not being satisfied, the obvious question would be: "Why am I not satisfied?"

Sense gratification is only furthering the distance to the desired state of satisfaction. To avoid the risk of public crucifixion, it should be mentioned that I don't mean to say that sex and sense gratification are forbidden or a sin. What I am trying to say is that they are not the answer, and that in our search for happiness we must find a higher taste.

SHORT SUMMARY

Pleasure is temporary and leads to frustration

*Pain in the beginning turns
to satisfaction in the end*

*If one is already satisfied,
there is no need for pleasure*

CHAPTER 7

Goals and priorities

"You gotta have a dream. If you don't have a dream, how are you gonna make a dream come true?"
- Oscar Hammerstein II, musician

The importance of a goal

In Alice in Wonderland there is a scene, which carries an important lesson for us. Alice in wandering through Wonderland, confused and bewildered. She doesn't know where she is, nor does she know where she is going. She meets a talking cat, which she asks in despair: "Can you tell me which way I should go?" The philosopher cat answers with a twinkle in the eye: "That depends on where you are going." "I don't know where I am going." Alice concedes. The cat smiles and exclaims: "Well, then it doesn't matter which way you go." The same holds true for us.

Where are you now?

First, we must have a sense of where we are. What is your situation right now? In other words, what are your skills and talents? What are your strengths and what are your weaknesses? What is your social situation? What does an average day look like? How is your health? What are your physical, emotional and financial resources, as well as your needs? Write it down to give yourself a bird's eye view. Where are you in life?

Where are you going?

The next point is your destination. It is interesting, that many don't have a defined goal in life. Try creating a survey with your friends and family: "What are your goals in life?" Those who can immediately present an answer that they have deeply thought about have much greater chances of success than those who are unclear.

Some make a philosophy out of not having defined goals and prefer "taking life as it comes." I cannot help but wonder if they really mean that. Maybe that could work in some cases where life unfolds like a Disney movie, but what if your philosophy leaves you homeless, lonely, and sick? I personally prefer having defined goals that I find meaningful and inspiring.

So it is wise to introspect: "What are my goals in life? What is the criterion of success for my existence? What is most important to me?" If this seems overwhelming, and your many goals are undefined, incoherent and pointing in all sorts of different directions, you may want to write them down on a paper.

If you know where you are, and you know where you want to go, the shortest distance between the two are a straight line. It becomes self-evident which way to go and what is required to make your dreams come true. If this is clear, and you're equipped with knowledge and the proper tools, then it is only time separating dreams and reality.

Kill your darlings

Those who have many, many goals are prone to not achieving any of them. The more things to be mindful of, the less you can focus on each. The more you embrace, the less you can squeeze. For the same reason parents send their children to private schools: too many students in the class means that the teacher cannot give each their full attention. It is the same with our many-branched desires. We may have to be selective, and acknowledge that some things are less important, and we shouldn't let those get in the way of the innermost desires of the soul.

Short-term and long-term

Try writing down all your goals in life on a list, and sort them in to short-term and long-term goals. A short-time goal could be passing an examination, a long-term goal could be to complete your education.

This list will give you an overview. Next, you should prioritize your long-term goals and mark them based on importance. For the time being, remove those of lesser importance. Remember that the more you embrace, the less you can squeeze.

Now that your long-term goals are condensed down to a few essential ones, you can go back to your short-term goals. The idea is to use your short-term goals as intermediate steps on the way toward attaining the long-term ones. See them as pearls on a string, and take them one at a time.

There is an interesting dynamic between situation and destination. If you have a destination and you take the required steps, the destination of today becomes the situation of tomorrow. Lets say you have a desire to get in shape, and you put the effort in, then you will get in shape. From situation to destination, work on it and repeat until you are where you want to be.

A big meal in small bites

I have a good friend who works with cows. He was once called from the barn in the middle of the night. A poor cow was lying on the floor choking on something. He hurried down to attend it. The cow was in panic, desperately trying to breathe. He calmed it, and reached his hand down the cow's throat, where he felt something that had got stuck. It turned out to be a big round potato.

A big goal can be overwhelming, and if you contemplate the project as a whole you may very well get discouraged, or attempt to swallow it all at once, only to find yourself choking on it. It is important to chew your potatoes: the same holds true for completing a grand task. A journey is but a series of steps. A book is read one page at a time. No one knows how the pyramids where build, but most likely laying one stone at a time. You should use the same progressive method to reach your goals.

The distance to the goal is not as important as our direction and pace. It doesn't matter if it's far away, as long as you're moving in the right direction. You cannot change the distance, but you can change your direction and pace, slowly but surely ascending whatever heights you are aiming at.

SHORT SUMMARY

Without a goal one is already lost

Too many goals causes indecision

Reach a big goal with small steps

CHAPTER 8

Rules for efficiency

"Efficiency is doing things right; effectiveness is doing the right things"
– Peter Drucker, Management Consultant

Self-discipline and efficiency

We want to do minimum effort and get the maximum result. In other words, we want to be efficient. But as Peter Drucker points out, there is efficiency and effectiveness, i.e. doing things right, and doing the right things.

With a strong self-discipline you can get more things done faster and better. Sounds good, but take note. One of the worst ways to waste your time is doing a good job that isn't required or maybe even be counterproductive. Catholic monk Thomas Merton said, "People may spend their whole lives climbing the ladder of success only to find, once they reach the top, that the ladder is leaning against the wrong wall." Stephen Covey adds: "If the ladder is not leaning against the right wall, every step we take just gets us to the wrong place faster."

Four levels of efficiency

"There are four classes: lazy intelligent, busy intelligent, lazy foolish, and active foolish. The active foolish is a fourth-class man. So at the

present moment they're very active, but they're all foolish. Therefore the world is in danger."
– Srila Prabhupada

Lazy intelligence

A lazy person doesn't want to endeavour needlessly. That doesn't necessarily mean that he is sleeping the day away without any accomplishment. A lazy intelligent person can be much more effective than a busy intelligent person. How so?

The lazy intelligent person is focusing on the essential. He only acts on what is important. Therefore he is not necessarily working more, but his work has greater impact. He consciously postpones things, which are not of vital significance. Warren Buffett, one of the richest men in the world, was once asked about his secret to success. He answered: "Simple. I just say no to everything that is not absolutely vital to me at the moment."

The lazy intelligent person is also a master of delegating. He needs hands free to manoeuvre and make moves. Therefore he is always trying to outsource less important tasks, not that he couldn't do them himself, but his time is better spend thinking.

Active intelligence

Effectiveness and efficiency – doing things right and doing the right things - is the primary difference between active and lazy intelligence. A person with active intelligence can be immensely productive and competent. He does things right and finds joy in his engagements but spends less time thinking and therefore makes the mistake of hacking at the wrong tree, thus wasting precious time.

An active intelligent person functions best under guidance of lazy intelligence. That is a strong combination. One has the vision, the other makes it happen.

The lazy fool

This type is hopelessly inefficient, but rather harmless. Mostly they are just ruining their own lives. As with the lazy intelligent person he does as little as he can get away with, but what he does is, however, a complete waste of time. He can easily spend a decade playing computer games in his parents' basement, and have no problem living as a parasite off the goodwill of others. He has no goals and therefore nothing worth working towards, except maybe for the next pizza. If this comes across with a tinge of disgust, it is only because it reminds me of the life I used to live.

How can such a person rise above his lazy existence? Through good company. Changing circles. He is dependent on someone from the outside compassionately throwing a rope. For those who are trying to help such a person, it is important to remember that throwing a rope is not enough. They have to grab the rope and hold on tight, desiring to get out. Otherwise they will remain where they are.

The busy fool

Once when I was travelling in India, I saw a monkey trying hard to destroy a traffic light. It didn't succeed, but the sight was highly amusing. That is a classic example of the busy fool.

His actions are pointless, often doing more harm than good, both for himself and others.

The advantage of the busy fool is his active nature. He doesn't need to be forced into activities. It is already going on. He just needs a helping hand and some guidelines. He needs a person telling him what to do, and how to do it.

If we want to be more efficient, lazy intelligence is the best platform to work from. Srila Prabhupada was once speaking about the importance of common sense, and to that a young man asked: "What if you don't have common sense?" The answer was straightforward: "Ask someone who has." If you know a master of lazy intelligence you can observe and learn from them, utilising the mind-set and attitude of the good disciple as previously discussed.

Pareto's law

The Italian economist Vilfredo Pareto first wrote about the 80/20 rule, or Pareto's Law, in 1895. It is a law unknown to many, despite the fact that it is seemingly all-pervading. Its utility is strikingly agreeable with Srila Prabhupada's concept of lazy intelligence.

The 80/20 rule

IIn a nutshell: the minority of causes account for the majority of effects. Wait, what? Pareto discovered through his studies of economy a natural balance of what he called "the essential few" and the "many trivial". He saw that 20% of the population possessed 80% of the wealth and influence. Later, he discovered that same principle applied wherever he looked.

20% of the customers are the direct cause 80% of sales. 20% of products account for 80% of profits. 20% of our clothes are worn 80% of the time. 20% of a carpet gets 80% of the wear. 20% of criminals are responsible for 80% of crime. 20% of drinkers drink 80% of the beer. 20% of our activities will yield 80% of our results! Keep that in mind.

The interesting point is that if you have a list of things you need to get done - let's call it a to-do list for innovations sake - one or two items on that list are more likely more important than the other eight put together.

Quality over quantity

It may take just as long, if not longer, to complete one of the many trivial tasks as it would be completing one of the essential few. But the difference is incomparable. One or two important tasks well done can give a much more substantial result than many tasks of lesser importance that would have required the same amount of time.

So what to prioritise? The answer is obvious: the essential few! Unfortunately, the tendency is that people often postpone the essential tasks that carry the potential of making a significant positive change in the lives of themselves and others. People busy themselves with trivial activities, which yield minimal results. A tragic pattern of wasted potential.

Persons, who are busy all day solving unimportant tasks without ever getting to the essential few can work harder and longer, run faster and yell louder, but they never manage to be as efficient as those who deal with the important tasks first, and then get to the less important later, maybe, if they don't forget about it.

Find the 20%

Whatever you do, whether you are a student, housewife or head of state, you have a plate full of things which need to get done every day. Take some time to reflect on your options. What are the essential few, and what are the many insignificant? What can I do now, which will add most value to my life and lives of others? Write it down.

Invest in the 20%

When you have identified the activities which are most worthy of your precious time, install them in your frontal lobes as your indisputable priorities. Make it a rule not to spend time on the many insignificant things before the essential few have been dealt with.

It is of importance to be sensitive, flexible and often rethink the situation. What is wildly important at present may not be so in a month from now. Our essential few are most likely going to change, so we need to be flexible and able to adjust to changing circumstances. Something might be essential now as a part of process, later to be replaced with something else at a later phase.

Find the balance and avoid extremes

It is easy to be efficient for a while, but if the long-term effect of our so-called efficiency is sleep deprivation, stress and failed relationships, then we aren't really being efficient, are we?

When I did military service a few years ago, we did various physical tests. One of them was the classic Cooper-test: how long can you run in 12 minutes? It was fun to see an overenthusiastic, aspiring soldier, eagerly taking the lead, leaving the rest of us in the dust. It didn't take long, however, before his tank was running on empty, and we overtook him one at a time, as he was laying at the wayside gasping for air. And so, the tortoise beat the hare. Life is a marathon, and not a sprint. Find your balance, and set a pace that you can work consistently with. If it is not working, adjust.

Balance in practice

It is paramount to the quality of life that we maintain good health. That means we must eat healthy, exercise regularly and rest sufficiently, so we don't burn out. It is absurd, that some people are not willing to spend time and money on their health. The fact is, if we are not willing to take time for our health, we must take time for sickness.

The same is applicable in every aspect of life. We must find the balance. "One cannot become a yogi if one eats too much or eats too little, sleeps too much, or does not sleep enough. One who is regulated in his habits of eating, sleeping, working and recreation can live happily by practice of yoga." – *Bhagavad-gita*

SHORT SUMMARY

Find out what makes the big difference

Abandon minor tasks and focus on the important

Find the balance and avoid extremes

---

2. PART

ACTION

"Vision without execution is just hallucination"
- Thomas Edison

The shortest distance between two points is a straight line. First part dealt with the first point, sambandha, and the required knowledge of our present position. Second part is about practical application, which in Sanskrit is called abhideya.

Abhideya is the line connecting the dots, bringing us from here to there, from our present position to our desired destination. We will go through efficient methods of strengthening our self-discipline and establishing good habits that promote personal development, which are self-perpetuating and uplifting in general.

I have focused on the best methods and habits that I have picked up from my training as a monk. It should be mentioned that I haven't discovered anything new. I went treasure hunting in the ancient wisdom of the East, while simultaneously studying successful modern personalities and the patterns and practices they have utilised to reach their respective goals, and then drawing parallels in-between.

I have attempted to pass on what I have learned through personal experience about self-discipline in the coming chapters. My intention is to equip the reader with relevant tools that can be used to construct a positive upward spiral of self-development. Where it will take us depends entirely on our determination, and to what degree we are willing to invest ourselves in the process.

I recommend that you read through the chapters once to get an overview and take note of what inspires you the most. Then you can re-read the chapters that are most relevant to you at present to conduct more scrutinizing and think about how to implement the ideas.

To become anchored in these practices has been a gradual process for me, which have been stretching over several years. So take it easy. You don't have to implement everything from day one. It is perfectly fine if you can start off with experimenting with one or two practices, and come back when you are ready for more. Enjoy!

CHAPTER 9

Stay fit for fight

"I hated every minute of training, but I said: Don't quit. Suffer now and live the rest of your life as a champion."
- Muhammad Ali

The self-disciplined athlete

It is hard to come about better examples of self-discipline than professional athletes who live and breathe for their sport. When we see an athlete in the heat of the battle act with admirable skill on the borderline of perfection, we see an event taken out of context. We see a result of continuous practice. What we don't see are the thousands of hours spent preparing for that moment, tireless determination, extreme dedication, blood, sweat and tears that have brought about the skill we so admire.

Innate talents and good genetics definitely do make a difference, but talents without practice will wither away like a plant without water. The determining factor is self-discipline, or in the words of soccer legend Pelé : "Success is no accident. It is hard work, perseverance, learning, studying, sacrifice and most of all, love of what you are doing or learning to do."

Maybe you have a strong desire to become a professional athlete, maybe not. But I guess you desire a good life and with that aim in mind, health is a major ingredient. It too requires self-discipline to maintain a healthy lifestyle, but luckily not as much as winning Tour De France.

The value of perseverance

It is not possible to achieve good health or a strong constitution in a few weeks or months. It requires patience and perseverance. Many envision a healthier lifestyle, but without the necessary self-discipline to overcome bad habits and develop good ones, it is not going to happen. It will remain simple wishful thinking.

A study of people who made fitness-related New Year's resolutions showed that 46% had failed to keep their resolution within half a year. It is alarming, but not surprising how bad we are at following up on our decisions. Another statistic shows that 67% of the members in gyms never use them! Why? Well, you get a nice card but still... We must assume that there is a desire to workout. Otherwise, why would one pay the membership fee? It is but another expression of the lack of self-discipline in the modern world.

If one manages to get into the routine of exercising regularly, this one habit will act as gateway to more further positive lifestyle choices. The tendency is that individuals who commit themselves to physical activities on a regular basis become better at controlling negative patterns such as overeating, smoking and various addictions. Obviously! Why would one work hard to strengthen one's health while simultaneously working on sabotaging it? It is equivalent to pouring water on a fire you are trying to light.

Good advice

I will not go through any workout plans here. There are many who are much more qualified to guide in this regard. Instead,

I will focus on generating a strong motive for getting into a good health routine, if you don't already have one. If you do, then I recommend that you start seeing your routine in relation to cultivating self-discipline.

Motivation

How to exercise depends on the 'why'. What is the motive? There is a big difference in working towards strength, endurance or flexibility, so be clear about your motive. Again, if you know where you are, and you know where you want to go, the path becomes self evident. If you are trying to become the world champion of dead lifting, you need something heavier than a skipping rope.

My own motive is well-being and optimal health. I want to stretch my youth for as far as possible. I want to live in body, which is functional, so that I may continue doing what I love without hindrance, also when I get old. My motivation is elderly hunchbacked people who have difficulties walking! I don't want to end up like that. They remind me why I exercise.

I enjoy comfortably sitting in a lotus posture, do headstands, touch my toes and stretch and twist my back and elongate my spine, not mention run, dance and go for long walks. I intend to keep it that way. Therefore I have a regimen of yoga exercises, which I am very enthusiastic about.

Physical and mental health

Physical exercise yields obvious benefits, as long as you don't get injured! It is good for the heart and blood circulation, strengthens muscles, bones and tissues, aids digestion and makes you look better. But there are also amazing by-products to physical activity that are often overlooked.

The brain coordinates the movements of the body. The neurologist Dr. Daniel Wolpert claims, that the main function of the brain is to manage bodily movements. He gives an example of a squid, which is living most of its life attached to a rock. As soon as it finds a suitable rock, it settles and starts digesting its own brain! His hypothesis is: the less we move, the less we require a brain. That can be an intimidating thought if you are living a stationary lifestyle, spending most of your time at the desk in front of a screen. Like a squid on a rock, digesting its own brain. Perhaps. It may sound like an exaggeration, but there is a clear connection between not getting enough exercise and neurological diseases like Alzheimer's, dementia and the like.

On the flip-side: the brain grows with movement. Dr. Wendy Suzuku, professor and neuroscientist at New York University, demonstrated that the brain grows in dimension and performance with regular exercise. Small miracles occur in both the prefrontal cortex and hippocampus when we engage in physical activity. According to the neurologists, the prefrontal cortex is accountable for personality, concentration, motivation, language, making decisions and much more. The hippocampus is primarily working with memories and remembrance.

The mental benefits of physical activity in and of themselves are so desirable that if we could manufacture a pill that would give the same results (stronger intelligence, learning ability, concentration and memory, mood enhancement, emotion management, reduction of stress, anxiety and depression, while significantly reducing the risk of physical and neurological diseases) it would, according to Dr. Mark Tranopolsky, be the most popular product of the medicinal industry.

Thank God we don't have to wait for modern science! Exercise is available for free, as granted by Mother Nature. It is easily available and in fact used to be a prerequisite for survival. If we want to reap the many benefits, it is recommended that we exercise a minimum of 30 minutes three times a week, and it should be challenging.

Schedule your workouts

Planning is always a good idea! More on that later, but for now: schedule your workouts and your resting days in before. Note them in your calendar or in a training log. Scheduling your workouts makes it easier to develop the habit.

It is liberating not having to deal with the whether or not to work out on a specific day. You just stick to the plan. A good workout plan is like a defence system against bad excuses, and makes it difficult for the mind to convince you to skip a day. It creates too much disturbance in the schedule: it is easier just sticking to the plan. It also feeds our self-discipline to make a plan and sticking to it, which is always good

Resting

Remember to be sensitive. Ignore your mind, but listen to your body. Keep your resting days sacred. Recovery is essential. Everyone is different and some recover faster than others. But a good general recommendation is working out three times a week with a day in between. For example Monday, Wednesday, Friday and then two rest days after a cycle.

It can be beneficial to take a rest week at intervals after a couple of months of steady commitment, if you feel like your body needs it. This provides an opportunity to recover thoroughly and you will often experience coming back stronger after a week's break.

Making exercise fun

It is important to like your routine, if you don't want to end up like those who are financing the gyms without ever using them. In that case, you may as well use your money to save the rainforests, provide food for the needy or supporting the local monks. You have to look forward to working out! It should relieve tension and function as a recreational element in life.

It doesn't have to cost anything. Gravity is our friend and nature has provided our bodyweight to work with. Yoga, calisthenics, parkour and many other forms of exercise are fun and free once you've got a hang of it.

I like sleeping on my yoga mat and do my routine in my pyjamas as the first thing in the morning when I wake up. That is smart! I am saving time by not having to change, and once I am damp and sweaty I am ready for a cold shower. That is an incomparably good way to start the day! You can workout at home on a mat, or run down to the local playground and do pull-ups and be creative with the facilities. Just be sensitive and try not to scare the children. Okay?

SHORT SUMMARY

Bad health can ruin an otherwise good life

*Create a lifelong health routine a
nd habits you love*

*Great benefits for the body, mind
and self-discipline*

CHAPTER 10

Discipline push-ups

"Sow a thought and you reap an action; sow an act and you reap a habit; sow a habit and you reap a character; sow a character and you reap a destiny." ."
– Ralph Waldo Emerson, American author and philosopher

One gains strength by doing push-ups. If not, no one would bother doing them. The stronger you get, the more you can take. Your capacity is growing. It is exactly the same thing that happens when you do a small thing that you don't feel like doing. You are overruling your mind and grow your self-discipline. With time, you will gradually be able to do greater things that you don't feel like doing.

It accumulates with compound interest and soon enough you will be able to move mountains. The increased self-discipline also increases the quality of life. You become more productive, self-confident, optimistic, healthier and happier. All good stuff. But one of the most sensational by-products is the taste that you get for activities that generate more self-discipline. You will start finding pleasure in refusing temptations and embracing inconveniences. It starts out as a tiny snowball, but quickly becomes an avalanche, an unstoppable force of nature.

The mutable brain

The comparison of physical exercise and exercising patterns of thought and behaviour is very appropriate. Neuroscience has now discovered that ours thoughts and deeds have a physical effect on the structure of brain. It is called neuro-plasticity.

That means if you begin regularly doing your discipline push-ups or in another way make a significant change in your conduct, doctors would be able to register that change if they were to scan the inside of your skull. Just as you can easily see that a person who is working out and living a healthy life has beautiful muscles, good posture and other symptoms of that lifestyle, you can see the many positive effects in the brain of a person who has good habits and a healthy mental state.

Embrace resistance

Resistance is necessary to build up self-discipline. If you stop pushing as soon as it gets uncomfortable, you will never get stronger. Ambitious individuals therefore deliberately seek challenges, or at least they welcome them to appear of their own accord, knowing well that they are a main ingredient in personal development.

Do first things first

In his book Eat That Frog! Brian Tracy explains the importance of solving the most essential tasks first, preferably early in the morning. The tendency is that we procrastinate the most important, as it is often the most demanding and intimidating. For instance, it is much easier to answer emails than turning in job applications.

But why would one postpone that which is going to have the greatest positive effect on ones life? We want that effect as soon as possible! As such, it is a good habit to discipline yourself to solving the most important tasks first, even though it might feel like eating a live frog. Brian Tracy has a good rule when it comes to eating frogs: if you are going to eat two frogs, start with the ugliest one.

It should be mentioned that I am vegetarian myself, and do not encourage the eating of innocent frogs. So don't take the frog eating too literally. Leave that to the French and go do something meaningful with your life instead. Okay?

Positive addiction

To complete an important task, especially early in the morning, leaves you feeling immensely satisfied and is a really good way to start your day. I am no scientist but the neurologists talk about reward circuit, the part of your brain that is in charge of making you feel good by releasing endorphins, dopamine and happy chemicals. This area of the brain generates energy, enthusiasm and confidence whenever you complete an important task, as a reward for your endeavour. What a bonus! This euphoric feeling can easily become a healthy addiction. Addiction is not always a bad thing. This addiction is based on doing what needs to be done. And so, you can exploit the reward system, getting naturally high on a daily basis, without needing to go rehab.

SHORT SUMMARY

Self-discipline can be strengthened as a muscle

See the opportunities in challenges

Learn to love what you hate, if it's good for you

CHAPTER 11

Think on paper

"Writing is thinking on paper."
- William Zinsser

Thoughts can be worth more than gold. Write them down! You are probably having hundreds of genius thoughts every single day, or at least some. We cannot know when our inner brilliance will awaken, so it's good to be prepared for when it does. Just the habit of keeping a notebook and a pen, for those divinely inspired moments can make all the difference in life.

To write down one's thoughts is a simple but clever way to keep your life organized and help you spend time efficiently. It is also a good tool to set goals and keep you mindful of your good ideas. The rare but meticulous bookkeepers write down their goals and accomplish many times more than those, who for some reason, never take the time to formulate their goals in writing.

The magic of the written word

When you write down a goal it becomes concrete. An idea or thought is abstract. But when that same idea is written on paper it becomes part of physical reality. In the Vedas, the development of reality is similarly described as moving from subtle to gross. When something is written it is tangible. It can be seen and felt. As soon as you engrave a goal in your notebook, you are one step closer to attaining it. If, on the other hand, it is left uncared for, it may hang around on the plane of fantasies and daydreams for a while before then being forgotten and merged into oblivion.

Clear goals have an amazing effect on one's consciousness, which will seek an inspiring goal as a heat-seeking missile follows a jet engine. If the inspiration is intense, the mind will continue the chase even while you're asleep! We all have the experience of waking up with clarity of purpose and a head full of good ideas. For the ambitious soul, the sub-consciousness is working wonders even as we sleep.

Plan every day

"Planning is bringing the future into the present so that you can do something about it now." - Alan Lakein. A lot of people wake up every day more or less disoriented. Few take time to make an exact plan for their activities on a daily basis. As the saying goes: "Failing to plan is planning to fail."

A good investment of time

An average westerner has a lifespan of approximately 81 years. That is 29.565 days. A huge percentage of our allotted time is spent sleeping, working, watching television and so on. And how much time does that leave us for living the lives that we want to live?

Time is a resource. We can reduce the amount of wasted minutes, hours and days by taking a bit of time, to plan our time, which will give us more time. You can plan your day in a couple of minutes; it doesn't take more than that. And this humble investment of minutes will be generously rewarded in hours.

Simple and genius

Planning is easy! Execution is the difficult part, but if we can start with getting the planning right, then so far so good. All that is required is a pen and a paper. That is all. It is the same principle whether you are using your smartphone, post-its or a notebook. You just make a list of all the things you are going to do before doing it.

It works wonders from day one. So just get started. Let the list be a magic carpet carrying you way beyond your previous capacity. Just remember, that your list is a servant. It is a tool, and shouldn't take control of your life. The goal is not to become a wretched workaholic, but developing your potential, so you can live a life worth living.

Be efficient with your time. Work, when you are working. Read, when you are reading. Exercise, when you are exercising, and be warm and affectionate when you are with the people you love. Your increased self-discipline should give you plenty of surplus energy to allow leniency with your schedule and leave time for deep relationships.

Different lists

The concept of different lists for different purposes is something I picked up from Brian Tracy. They nicely support a self-disciplined lifestyle and have catalysed many little miracles in my life. As a matter of fact, they helped me write this book. So I thought I would share that with you.

Previously we discussed goals and priorities. By now, you should have clearly defined your goals and written them down. If not, this is good time to do so. Put down the book for a while and get thoughtful. Dig into your brain and heart for inspiring ideas and write them down on paper. What are you passionate about? What are your innermost desires? What would you like to accomplish in this life? This is your life's to-do list.

The to-do list of life

Don't worry, it can be changed down the road. In fact it is recommended to contemplate and refine your goals and priorities as you go, keeping in mind why you do what you do. The list of life can seem overwhelming. But that is good! It means that you are ambitious and think big. That makes life exciting and challenging. If your list is not wildly ambitious, that is great too. Maybe you're not so passionate and focused on external achievements. We are all different and there should be room for that. But if you have big dreams, then you will do well to break them up into manageable parts and for that, the other lists come in handy.

A list for every month

How much can you do in a month? Much more than you think, if you start with thinking. What can you do this month, to close in on your dreams? Again, there are so many trivial and unimportant things that somehow enter our lives and distract us. They should not be allowed to remove the focus of the essential few things that will make the big difference.

If you have a desire to say, write a book, as I am doing right now, then set yourself an intermediate goal for this month and prioritise it. That could be studying a branch of the subject, finishing a portion of the book or preparing the marketing campaign.

Stay conscious of your life's list, and see every month in connection to that. Make sure you are doing little things on a daily basis that will yield the big result. There is an Indian saying that tiny droplets eventually fill a bucket. That is also called the compound effect. Use it. Start every month with looking at your life's list, and think about you can do this month, and then add that to your monthly list.

A list for every week

Same procedure as above. Divide the points of the monthly list in smaller portions and add them to the weekly list. Less important things will surface as you go through each week, see to them, but don't let them distract you to the extent that you lose the connection to your life's list.

A list for every day

Last but not least, transfer points from the monthly and weekly to a daily list. Make the list every evening. You can start with adding the things you didn't manage to complete today. When you go to bed after writing your list, you are almost guaranteed to wake up inspired.

Always work from a list and tick away each task as you finish it. This will generate a feeling of steadfast progress and at the end of the day, week or month you can look back and see how much ground you've covered. This will inspire you to keep moving, and raise your level of ambition next time you write your list, as you witness your innate potential gradually unfold.

The ABCD method

Here is another time-management nugget from Brian Tracy. You will have a lot of points on your list, and some are more important than others. Therefore you need a system to prioritise them. That is the purpose of this method. This is how it works: when you have made your list for tomorrow's activities, you write A, B, C, D or E, in the margin next to each point.

A's are very important. Those are the things that will have the greatest positive effect on your life if done nicely and, reversely, have major negative consequences if neglected. These are things you must do.

If you put an A next to a point you commit to it. Prioritizing something and then disregarding it is a bad habit and is harmful to your self-discipline. Just be aware of that. If you have more than one A-task, you can further categorize them "A1", "A2", "A3" and so on.

B's are also important, but less than the A's. You can neglect a B-task without it being a catastrophe. That doesn't mean they should be neglected, but they shouldn't be prioritized over an A-task. If at the end of the day you've crossed your B's but the A's are left standing something went wrong. Remember to put first things first.

C's are not so important. They don't make a big difference. It is something that would be nice to do, but which is more or less redundant. C's can be postponed or eliminated if you don't find time, or feel like doing it anyway.

D's are things that should be delegated. We touched upon delegation in the chapter on efficiency, where the lazy intelligent person was praised for the ability to delegate and empower others to take care of less important issues so he can focus on the essential.

The combination of the monthly, weekly and daily lists allied with the ABCD-method is a pre-eminent tool in a self-disciplined existence. What makes the big difference is disciplining oneself to get started with and finishing the A1 tasks as soon as possible. Since they will have the greatest effect one will naturally experience a corresponding reward for one's endeavour. When you are done postponing your A1's and get to work with determination, you will experience accomplishing more than you could previously have imagined!

KORT OPSUMMERING

Make a habit of writing down good ideas

*Time spent planning comes
back with an interest*

Plan days, weeks and months in advance

CHAPTER 12

A smart investment

*"If we encounter a man of rare intellect, we
should ask him what books he reads"*
- Ralph Waldo Emerson

The importance of reading

Imagine having access to the world's greatest minds and personalities. From the ancient Greek to the European philosophers, kings and generals, scientific geniuses, the self-realised
souls of the East, successful entrepreneurs and Olympic athletes. Imagine you could choose whomever you would like
to spend some time with. You could talk with them, observe
and learn from them. The good news is that you can: who
they were, what they thought and how they lived has been
immortalised in the written word. By regularly reading good
books you can literally come in direct contact with the most
amazing and influential persons in history. Reading as such is
one of the most transformative habits we can possibly adopt.

Jim Rohn once made the claim that you are the average of
the people you spent the most time with. By reading good books
by great authors you are raising that average considerably. The
Vedas give the analogy that an iron rod in a fire gradually warms
up until the point of becoming red hot. If you then put that same
rod in a pile of dried twigs and leaves, they will burst into flames.
The iron will acquire the burning quality of the fire by close contact. In a similar way, we are product of our surroundings.

Maybe you cannot eat lunch with your hero but you can read his book, and that is almost as good, if not better! One of my favourite authors A.C. Bhaktivedanta Swami Srila Prabhupada once said: "My books are better than me, because I have invested the best of myself in my books."

So what are we waiting for? We have a unique possibility to associate with the most remarkable personages that have ever walked the earth. With the good habit of reading substantial literature, you cannot help but becoming a more substantial person.

Rekindling the appetite for knowledge

There are many benefits derived from immersing oneself in good literature. Unfortunately many stop reading as soon as they finish their formal education. That is a shame. Education should never stop. Not that everyone should necessarily become an academic or a scholar, that is not what the world needs. But education in one way or another must continue, and at a certain time we have to become responsible for it ourselves.

The appetite for knowledge is like a fire, and knowledge in the form of books, lectures and documentaries are like fuel to flames. The fire grows as you add firewood, and its capacity to burn grows with it. But be careful with overloading the fire or adding wet wood, as it may extinguish the flames.

That is the often the paradoxically unwanted result of the modern system of education. It suffocates our curiosity! What a crime. Somebody call the Human Rights Committee! As children of mankind, the hope for the future, we should preferably graduate from school with our desire for knowledge not merely alive, but fuelled with inspiration for a lifetime of continuous learning.

But the fact is many have their appetite slaughtered on the alter of institutionalized education. I meet a lot of people who confess to not having opened a book since primary school. I was in that category myself. I first started studying seriously after finishing my education. Finally I felt free to study what inspires me. And my appetite gradually reawakened. So what do you do if the educational system traumatised out of reading?

A humble beginning

Just to sit down and open a book can be intimidating if you are not used to it. So don't make it harder than it is already. Start with books at a manageable size, which are sufficiently interesting to keep you inspired throughout.

A couple of pages every day is a good start. Just get into the habit. As the taste develops, you will become more ambitious and gradually start reading literature at a higher level or more books at a time.

The daily dose

How much to read is up to the individual. Warren Buffet was once again all about the key to success. He pointed to a stack of books and said: "Read 500 pages like this every day," while reaching toward a stack of manuals and papers. "That's how knowledge works. It builds up, like compound interest." Bill Gates reads a book a week. Elon Musk was once asked how he learned to build rockets. His answer? "I read books." Thousands of years ago the sage Canakya Pandit said: "As tiny droplets eventually fill a bucket, so also should knowledge, virtue and wealth be gradually accumulated."

So what is the daily dose? That is individual. But it is good to set a standard and stick to it. Personally I feel malnourished if I don't read a book a week. All it takes is an hour a day to devour a medium size book a week. That accumulates to more than 50 books in a year. That's quite something. But still, you can't read everything, so you have to be selective.

Quality over quantity

Bruce Lee once remarked: "I fear not the man who has practised 10,000 kicks once, but I fear the man who has practised 1 kick 10,000 times." Don't think of a book as a one-night stand! Think of a book as a friend. As a person you can have a relationship with. You don't need a million friends. You need good friends. Same thing with books.

If you read, re-read and study your favourites you become familiar with them in a different way than with books you only read once. You can read them with a marker and highlight important passages. That makes them easier to read the next time around. Then you can skim through them later and quickly find the passages that you are looking for. I personally fill my favourites up with notes, stickers and memorize inspiring passages.

Try collecting 10, 20 or 30 good books over time – as many as you feel comfortable with. But read them regularly, not necessarily cover to cover, but at least go through the highlights at intervals. In that connection C.S. Lewis said:

"It is a good rule after reading a new book, never to allow yourself another new one till you have read an old one in between."

Avoid distractions

There is a world of difference between focused reading, being fully absorbed, and reading in a distracting environment. So you'd do well to take some precautions. The best guarantee for a peaceful reading session is to start before the world wakes up. You can also put your phone on flight mode with the screen facing downwards or at a safe distance, so you don't feel tempted to pick it up. Some like to listen to music as they read. I personally prefer silence when I read, and for that a good earplug and a 'don't disturb sign me' are a couple of powerful allies.

Study companions and book clubs

To talk about what you've read increases the chances that it will move from your short- to long-term memory. If reading a book is like eating a meal, then reflecting, discussing and explaining is the process of digestion that enable us to absorb nutrition from our meal.

Sometimes it is said that you are what you eat. But that is not true. You can eat all the best stuff in the world, but if your digestion is failing, then what is the use? You are not what you eat. You are what you digest! So don't just read good books, unless you are just looking for entertainment. If you want to grow as a person, make a conscious effort to assimilate and activate what you read.

SHORT SUMMARY

Make a habit of reading good books

Set a minimum of pages to read every day

Re-read your favourites often

CHAPTER 13

The power of vows

"There is one prevailing key to success. Do what you resolve to do. Then you'll be a success. If you can discipline yourself to follow through on your promises to yourself, your self-esteem goes up. Persistence is self-discipline in action. Self-discipline is the foundation of self-confidence"
– Brian Tracy

It is fascinating, that in the Danish language the word 'vow' is 'løfte', which literally means to lift. That is interesting. By taking and keeping a vow you are lifting yourself! You lift your integrity! You lift your self-discipline! Taking a vow, and strictly adhering to it is a wonderful practice for building self-discipline.

It is a matchless opportunity to test your vigilance, will power and patience. But start with something small. Before you go and promise someone that you will love them to death do you apart, then first prove to yourself that you can stick to your word. Empty promises don't count.

Little vows

It is easier to complete a vow with a deadline. Well obviously, vows without an expiry dates are never really completed. But still, set a date and you have something you can focus your mind on. Upon completing your vow, the reward centre in your brain will go nuts. Also, if you are having withdrawal symptoms on the third day of a chocolate-fast, and you vowed to abstain for a week, then it is calming to know, that there is light at the end of the tunnel.

I like monthly vows. It helps me defining the borderline need and greed. It is said, that you don't notice your shackles until you start moving. If you vow not to touch your phone or go on Facebook for a week, you will find out how addicted you are.

Little vows also give you a great chance to enrich your life by adding a positive element, or removing a negative one, and find out what that feels like. If you like it, stay with it. As such, a little vow can turn out to add permanent value to your life.

From vow to lifestyle

I once took a vow to eat one meal a day for a month. It began with a book by Canakya Pandit. Canakya claims that a wise person is satisfied with one meal a day. "A wise person" I thought, "That sounds just like me!" Seeing my ego being contested, I had to try it.

The first couple of days were challenging. The body is used to a certain pattern, and if we usually eat at fixed times, the body will protest if we skip a meal. But do we have to eat, as soon as the tummy rumbles? What is hunger anyway, and what goes on in the body when we experience it?

The physio- and psychological benefits of fasting are awfully fascinating. Therefore I have dedicated the next chapter to go in-depth with the subject. But this part is about vows, so let's stick with that before moving on.

The point is that making a vow doesn't just lift your self-discipline and integrity. You get the opportunity to experiment with and enhance your lifestyle. I learned a lot about my body and mind during that month. That vow has now become an integrated part of my lifestyle. I've been eating one meal a day for more than a year. And if I occasionally eat twice in a day, it is only for social purposes. My body functions way better with one meal. Why? We'll get to that.

A FEW SUGGESTIONS FOR VOWS

Honesty

A study conducted at Massachusetts University in 2002 demonstrated that 60% of their adult subjects couldn't keep a 10-minute conversation without lying. Most of us lie and are lied to every single day. Another interesting study from Notre Dame University showed that people who tell fewer lies generally have better relationships, for obvious reasons, experience less stress and anxiety and even have better health!

Many of us lie because we are insecure. But it is a bad solution to remediate your insecurity, because now you have to keep track of your lies, and remember who you've told what. It is easier and more dignified to just be an honest reliable person.

Suggestion: try to go for a week or a month without telling a lie. You are more than welcome to continue indefinitely. But there is really nothing to lose except for guilt and bad conscience.

Abstinence

It is common knowledge, that drinking alcohol is killing brain cells, and smoking causes cancer, but despite the obvious negative consequences of our many addictions, they are to a large degree an ingrained part of modern culture. In Denmark where I am from, it would be considered a real accomplishment for a young person to stay sober for a weekend. Abstinence requires self-discipline, but the benefits are self-evident.

For me personally to quit intoxicants marked the beginning of self-development, increased productivity and a better life. I realised self-purification of body and mind, which resulted in greater well-being, and I consequently reversed many of my addictions. It became a positive obsession for me to replace bad habits with good ones, which saved me time, money and health. Sometimes people ask me if I miss anything, the answer is a firm "no!" I am so glad I am through with hangovers from intoxicants most of all.

Suggestion: try to go for a week or a month abstaining from an addiction. Whether it is smoking, drinking, overeating, playing computer games, most people have something that they are struggling with. Free yourself! Find a higher taste! Start with a week, and notice the difference. It is not so difficult. You can do it!

Celibacy

I used to think living without sex was impossible. That the need was so fundamental to us, and the desire so strong, that to not act on it would surely drive one mad.

After researching the subject, it turns out the scientific investigation of celibacy is very limited. It is also hard to find subjects these days who can actually practice celibacy without their rampant sexual desires provoking wet dreams and involuntary ejaculations after a couple of weeks. The modern scientific community is consequently quite ignorant about the effects of celibacy on the human body and mind. However, the timeless wisdom of the East glorifies celibacy and the effect it has on us physically, mentally and spiritually.

But now we are talking about self-discipline and not human anatomy. Having lived in celibacy for six years I can safely say that there is no better test of self-discipline. Half the definition of self-discipline is being able to refrain from acting on your desires. What could be a better test then?

Many great thinkers like Isaac Newton and Nikola Tesla were celibate. Muhammad Ali abstained from sex for weeks and months before an important fight. His coach said his abstinence was the key to his success. Many top athletes follow his example.

Suggestion: I am convinced that it would be good for anyone to regularly take a vow of celibacy. I am not saying you should become a monk or a nun, but try at intervals to go for as long as you can. Or as an alternative, if this is asking too much, you can avoid pornography for some time. The idea is to control the sex impulse. If you can do that, the world is yours!

Vegetarianism

I once met a Muslim who was fasting during Ramadan. I asked her if she couldn't abstain from meat also, while she was at it. I proposed she do it as an experiment and afterwards have a serious one-on-one talk with God upon completing the fast, asking Him if it was a good addition to her religious practice. The idea was that she should be vegetarian for a month, but something happened and now she is a full-time herbivore. Here's a great example of a little vow turning into a lifestyle.

I personally became vegetarian in the military when a friend sent me a documentary about the health benefits of a vegetarian diet. The Air Force Training Centre had a nice canteen and so I could easily make the transition without having to re-learn how to cook. The advantages came quickly. After a month I beat many of my personal fitness records in speed, strength and endurance (not that I am particularly strong, but I was quite fast back then). I felt happier, healthier and much more alert. For me, that was all the evidence I needed to keep going.

Suggestion: Try living as a vegetarian for a month and then see how you feel. If you feel better than ever and you don't crave meat, then just go ahead and continue. It's good for you, the animals and the planet. If it doesn't work out, you can always go back. But then you've made a conscious choice based on personal experience rather than just following the norms of society.

Cold showers and ice baths

How about getting out of your comfort zone first thing in the morning? Sounds horrible? That's why it's such a nice practice! Studies have shown, that momentarily exposing yourself to intense cold has numerous amazing side effects. It increases your blood circulation and oxygen intake, strengthens the immune system, alleviates and wards off depression, and has numerous other bodily and mental benefits. And for our purposes, it is an effective tool for building self-discipline.

Suggestion: Try to take a cold shower for a week or, if available, go winter bathing. Again, if it's too much, you can adjust. You may want to start with a warm shower, before ending with a long cold rinse. But going straight for the cold is the first choice.

Watch your mouth

A vow of complete silence could be interesting, but that is not what I have in mind. Some people constantly complain about their problems, the weather or the idiots running the government. Sound like you? I have these tendencies myself. But that is not really what the world needs. That is not what the people around you need. People don't care about your problems. There is enough negativity out there already.

Suggestion: Try not to complain about anything. Start with a week. If you can handle that, try to internalise it: don't just stop voicing your complaints, stop thinking your complaints. Have a renaissance within your mind. Focus on the good rather than the bad. Emphasize the positive and be indifferent to the negative. I once heard a monk say people are like flies and like bees. Flies are attracted to excrement, bees like flowers. Which one are you?

These are just suggestions. You don't have to follow. But my experience tells me that it can be both fun, rewarding and worthwhile to regularly take vows. You can start with a new one every week or month. Trust me on this, if you regularly take vows and complete them, you will very soon see some big positive changes in your life.

SHORT SUMMARY

Keeping promises to oneself is powerful

Taking a vow can change one's life

Take new vows regularly, pushing your limits

CHAPTER 14

To eat or not to eat

"Everyone can perform magic, everyone can reach his goals, if he is able to think, if he is able to wait, if he is able to fast"
- Hermann Hesse, Siddharta

What is fasting?

Fasting is abstaining from food and drink for medicinal, experimental or religious purposes. It is a practice that cannot be underestimated in the cultivation of self-discipline! We want food, and to control that want is self-discipline. Without self-discipline fasting is impossible.

But why say no to food? We have to eat to live, don't we? True. But how much do we need, and how often? And what happens in the body, when we don't eat?

Don't you die from that?

Yes, at some point. But not right away. Back in 1973, researchers at the University of Scotland monitored a man who fasted for 382 days. He would only take water, vitamins and minerals. When he started, he weighed in at 207 kg and 382 days later he finally reached his ideal weight of 82 kg and then he started eating again. So no worries, you are not going to die from skipping a meal or two.

Giving the body a break

To fast is first and foremost giving the stomach a break. How would you feel, if all life was just work, work, work? No pauses. No resting days. No vacations. Who said stress? Every single meal is putting your stomach to work. Many will never consider their tired digestive organs and mercilessly continue gulping up food all day every day.

Your stomach deserves a break, and giving it that will aid the body's natural healing processes. Don't underestimate the human body! It is a genius machinery. Nature has provided it with everything it needs to maintain good health. But it needs peace to do so.

A wound needs time to heal. If you are constantly playing with it, you are disrupting the process of recovery. It is the same thing with an injury. If you have sprained your angle, you need to stop walking on it. Why would it be any different with the body's internal affairs?

Why don't we hear more about it?

The food industry is the largest money machine in the world. Fasting is free and to propagate knowledge of its benefits is a serious threat to some very influential people's economical interest. Just imagine if hundreds of millions of people realized that they could live nicely, maybe even better on one meal a day, instead of three plus snacks. It would be the greatest catastrophe for the consumerist economy. One could also mention the conflict of interest in the medicinal industry, which is thriving on the poor health of the population, but I will summon my self-discipline and stick to the message.

Physiological advantages

It is not an exaggeration to say the advantages of fasting are miraculous. This section could easily take up a big portion, but my intention is to keep to book short and concise, so I have to provide just two scientific examples, which I find fascinating and inspiring.

Autofagi

Have you heard about self-eating? It might sound a bit cannibalistic in a strange egocentric way. But autofagi or self-eating is one the most revolutionary breakthroughs in health research in recent years. It might sound like an overstatement, but nonetheless Yoshinori Ohsumi received the Nobel Prize in 2016 for the ground breaking discovery.

Autofagi is the cells' ability to eat themselves. Why is that good? Envision a house with a magic box. Try to imagine, if you could throw old, useless and broken things into this box, which would then recycle them into new, useful materials, which could be used for renovating and face-lifting the place. That is exactly what autofagi does.

If there is no food in the stomach, the body will start searching for alternatives. The body is an intelligent machine. The first thing it breaks down is all the stuff you need the least: old cells, dead tissues, virus, bacteria, toxins and inflammation. As such, hunger necessitates an anatomical cleanse.

Think about that the next time your tummy is rumbling. Just let it do so. You are not going to die. Don't worry. Being hungry is good. Activate your self-discipline. Abstain. Let the thought of eating your own excess dead-weight be a source of inspiration.

Human growth hormone

One of the most common objections to fasting is, being afraid of losing muscle. What if you want to become strong and live in active life? Then you will have to eat quite often, right?

Good question. The hormone somatotropin, which is commonly known as HGH (human growth hormone) is what makes us grow. It helps us maintain muscle mass, form new muscle fibres, recover after exercise, strengthen tissues and bones, and heal after injuries. Sounds good, no?

Studies show, that the production of HGH increases with up to 2,000% in a fasted state. This increase starts 13 hours after the last meal and gradually rises up to 2,000%. Because of that, many athletes swear by intermittent fasting.

The Japanese acrobat Kohei Uchimura has won three Olympic gold medals, and four times silver. He works out twice a day on an empty stomach and is regarded by many as being the greatest gymnast of all time. We could give other examples of MMA fighters and American football players, people who are much stronger and way more active than you and me, but who are doing fine on one meal a day. So don't worry. You can fast, get the benefits, and be strong all at the same time.

Psychological advantages

Our bodies are designed for survival. If our existence is threatened by hunger, our cognitive function increases. Why? So we can find a solution to our hunger problem! Fasting therefore enables us to function at peak performance physically and mentally.

For this reason, many athletes prefer working out, fight and compete on an empty stomach. Not just athletes but inventors, presenters and students - all kinds of people that have realized that they are the best version of themselves when they are fasting. We have all experienced eating a big meal and then feeling completely drained afterwards. So if you have something important to do, you might want to postpone your meal until afterwards.

The science is rather complex so I will leave that for those who know better. Feel free to research it on your own. But even more important, try it out for yourself and gain some personal experience. The worst thing that can happen is that you will save money.

Intermittent fasting

Fasting at intervals is called intermittent fasting. The way to do it is by having scheduled timings for eating and fasting. I have given three examples of different ways to do that.

You can do intermittent fasting every day or every now and then. But it should be mentioned that the body likes routines. Start by doing some experiments, find out what works for you, and work with it. Your body will thank you later.

16:8

A 16-hour fast with an eight hour eating window is one of the most popular types of intermittent fasting. It is a good place to start. It is a mild form of fasting, which is not as physically or mentally demanding as some of other models.

The fast starts with the last meal of the day and is broken

16 hours later. As soon as the fast is broken, the eight hour eating window is opened, and you can eat as you like. If for example, one's last meal is at 16.00 in the afternoon, then the window will open again at 08.00 next morning.

You decide the timings yourself. The important point is to give your body 16 hours of fasting, so that the advantageous processes can work their magic.

20:4

This form of fasting is also known as "the warrior diet". Rumour has it that Roman soldiers and gladiators would fast throughout the day. It is sensible not having to eat or go to the toilet when you are in the Colosseum fighting for your life. In the evening, they would then have large feasts, which is why the "warrior diet" is operating on a four hour eating window. It is recommendable for athletes to use this type of fasting, eating in the evening, so that one can work on an empty stomach throughout the day.

23:1

Among yogis this is known as ekaharena, being satisfied with one deal a day. But it has not caught on in the modern world and most people know it as OMAD (one meal a day). This is the most intense of the intermittent fasts. But it is also much more efficient than the 16:8 and 20:4 models.

The 23:1 plan is first of all giving the body a 23 hours a day to take full advantage of autofagi, excretion of somatotropin and all the good stuff in the brain. Secondly, it is very kind on the stomach. It is quite manageable for the stomach only having to deal with one meal, just like it is always nice to leave early from school and work.

The risk is always not getting enough nutrition. You only have one meal to get all your calories, carbs, fat, proteins, vitamins, amino-acids and minerals. But generally the problem with nutrition is not quantity but quality, so just make sure to eat healthy, compensate with supplements, and you should be good.

Full fasting

Another option is not to eat anything throughout the day and going to bed on an empty stomach. This allows for the body to reach deeper levels of purification and get more into the healing processes. But it is more demanding and shouldn't be practised as often as the intermittent fasts. It is a good idea to plan a full fast in advance, in order to prepare mentally.

In the old Vedic culture of India it was custom to fast every second week on Ekadasi, which is the 11th day after new moon, and 11th day after full moon. Why? It is a little technical, but just in case you are considering a full fast, you might as well do it on Ekadasi. It is said to bring good fortune in many ways. Who knows, maybe they knew something we don't?

SHORT SUMMARY

Fasting can be great for one's health

It saves time, money and builds self-discipline

Experiment, and see what works for you

CHAPTER 15

Meditation

"From wherever the mind wanders due to its flickering and unsteady nature, one must certainly withdraw it and bring it back under the control of the self." – Bhagavad-gita.

Despite its growing popularity in the modern world, meditation remains a mystery for many. There are many myths and misunderstandings, and so my intention is to demystify the concept and provide elementary knowledge and inspiration, to either start or improve one's practice.Hvorfor meditere?

Why meditate?

There are so many big and small gains from meditation. What I am giving here are just a few samples, but hopefully enough to invoke some curiosity and excitement.

Knowledge of self

The first and foremost benefit of meditation is self-awareness, and practical acquaintance of human psychology, primarily our own. The mind and the nature of consciousness is the object for this awesome self-study, which is very relevant to anyone who sells the value of cultivating self-discipline.

When you meditate, you observe your thoughts and emotions. You see how restless and disturbed the mind is, and how it moves. Knowing of the patterns of thought and emotions comes in handy each and every day, for those who are aware of them. This awareness of the thought processes helps us to register unwanted thoughts and emotions, initial responses born out of the more unsophisticated part of the brain, and deal with them accordingly before they entangle us in a network of troubles.

Being able to distance yourself from your thoughts and observe them without judgement can be amusing and terrifying as well. It is like taking a sample of your consciousness. What you find might be shocking. But if you can tell yourself: "I am a crazy person!" that is a sign that you are making progress. Now you know what you're dealing with.

A transportable sanctuary

Once you've learned to meditate, you will always have a sanctuary within yourself, which you can use to cope with various stressful situations. Just close your eyes for a moment, breathe deeply and as the Bhagavad-gita says, bring the mind under the control of the self. Find some peace of mind, release some tension, and set your intention for what you are about to do, then step out again and deal with world.

Find your centre

Situations arise, where you loose your equilibrium. When that happens, you can practice restraining the mind before your emotions start running wild. Cars are rated on their acceleration from 1 to 100 km/h, but meditation is not about acceleration. It is about slowing down and finding tranquillity. That is an amazing ability. We cannot control what happens around us, but if we can control the mind, we can consciously decide how we will respond.

What does science have to say?

Despite meditations having been used for millennia, modern science has only just recently discovered its potential. But by now the advantages are already documented and established as scientific facts. Here are three amazing facts:

1. Meditation alters the structure of the brain positively

Studies show that regular meditation can reshape the brain. This is a concept called neuro-plasticity. The changes involve positive effects of memory, concentration and awareness. Dr. Andrew Newberg has been doing fMRI brain scans on practitioners of meditation for decades. The conclusion of his research is that regular meditators have significantly healthier brains than those who don't, and that they have a more satisfactory overall experience of existence.

2. Meditation can reduce stress, anxiety and depression

It has been proven that meditation can efficiently reduce one's level of stress and that it alleviates anxiety and depression. That is old news for those who meditate, but some people will never believe anything until it's on National Geographic.

Stress is the soundtrack to the modern world. It is the most common mental illness today. In Denmark, every fifth Dane has been on sick leave due to stress in the last five years.

The numbers are slightly varying but quite similar through-out the Western world. The number of children and teenagers diagnosed with stress and anxiety has tripled within the last 10 years. If we consider how exposed modern man is to these illnesses and how effectively meditation counteracts that, one might wonder why it is not given greater emphasis?

3. Meditation can improve your relationships

It was recently discovered that meditation affects areas in the brain that are connected with empathy and compassion. In the Bhagavad-gita there is a beautiful verse stating that the true yogi sees the happiness and distress of others as his own. In other words, he is deeply emphatic and compassionate upon other living beings. He rejoices in their happiness and feels their pain.

When this genuine empathy is combined with the emotional stability and the surplus energy that comes as a by-product of meditation, one becomes better at relating to others and caring for them. Thus, relationships naturally improve.

MYTHS ABOUT MEDITATION

You are supposed to stop your thoughts

It is a misunderstanding that one must not think of anything when meditating. It must result in thinking about not thinking, and that is still thinking. One cannot stop thinking at any point, and trying will be frustrating. The conclusion will be "This doesn't work for me", "I am not good at this", and thus one will quit. You need a focal point on which to anchor your concentration and control your mind from wandering. It may be your breath, an emotion such as gratitude or a mantra.

With a focal point, one can notice when the mind drifts off and then lovingly bring it back like a parent brings the child on proper course. As the Bhagavad-gita states: "From wherever the mind wanders to its flickering and unsteady nature, one must certainly withdraw it, and bring it back under the control of the self."

You have to sit on the floor

The point of sitting cross-legged or in a lotus posture is that it's good for keeping the spine erect and a good posture supports concentration. But if you are not used to sitting on the floor, then the discomfort will be more of a distraction than a support, and so it would be better to sit comfortably on a couch or a soft chair as you are meditating. Just try not to sink in and fall asleep.

Meditation isn't for me

I heard this one many times. People say they cannot concentrate and therefore meditation isn't for them. That is no excuse! Especially those who have a hard time concentrating should meditate. The mind is disturbed and that is what meditation will help them with. We learned to walk, talk, read and write. With some practice we may also learn to control the mind. Take it from someone whose mother was convinced he had ADHD, and has now been meditating two hours every single day for the last six years.

The benefits are too many and too good for you to disqualify yourself for whatever reason! At least, that is my humble opinion. If you are up for the challenge, keep reading, as we'll explore three kinds of meditation.

There are many traditions using various methods. How one meditates depends on which system one uses and from whom you learn it. I will discuss three variations which have worked for me, and that you can experiment with yourself.

1. Breath meditation

As mentioned, we need a focal point for our meditation, and the breath is an obvious choice. Breathe through your nose. It is healthier and more natural. Inhale deeply and slowly, trying to stretch each breath, filling up the diaphragm, then the lungs, widening the chest, hold it for some time nourishing your cells with delicious oxygen before letting go in a relaxed yet forceful exhalation.

It may seem unnatural at first, but that's just because we've now become accustomed to the unnatural, being conditioned by artificial standards of living, seeing everything upside down. Get familiar with deep breathing, and let the rhythmical breath be your focus. Feel the air moving through your nostrils into the lungs and move to the different parts of the body, withdrawing your attention from the external world. After some time, you will start to feel very relaxed and calm.

Previously we discussed discipline push-ups. That is also a natural by-product of meditation. At one point the mind will rebel: "Now I am done! Let's do something else. Stand up and let's get going." The challenge then is continuing. Ignore the mind and go a little further. Muhammad Ali once said,

"I don't count my sit-ups; I only start counting when it starts hurting, because they are the only ones that count." Not that meditation should be painful, but if we want to build self-discipline then we should go beyond the point when the mind concedes.

2. Mantra-meditation

Another great option is meditating on the sound of mantra. The word mantra is a Sanskrit word that means to free the mind. Sound affects our consciousness, as has been experienced by anyone listening to music. We utilise that principle with mantra-meditation, by exposing the mind to a positive and uplifting sound vibration. The sound of a mantra is designed to control the mind as a snake charmer controls a snake by the sound of his flute. There are many different mantras. I use this one:

Hare Krishna Hare Krishna
Krishna Krishna Hare Hare
Hare Rama Hare Rama
Rama Rama Hare Hare

This mantra is composed of names of God in Sanskrit. In the Vedas it has been described that God has a masculine and a feminine aspect. Krishna is the masculine, Hare is the feminine counterpart and Rama is the highest pleasure, which is said to be experienced in the loving service of God. As such, this mantra is more than a meditation-aid, which helps you to focus the mind. It is a prayer. A personal address to Krishna through his names, recited with concentrated loving devotion. Very beautiful. Traditionally you would receive the mantra from a spiritual master, and that is still recommended for authenticity's sake, but just to get you started, you might want to make a YouTube search for proper pronunciation.

If one is an atheist and has a reservation about reciting Krishna's names, one can use any other mantra. But again, if one doesn't believe in God, then Hare Krishna is supposedly just a sound amongst many other sounds, so then what is the problem?

It is simple. All you have to do is recite the mantra and listen to it. That is the external practice, internally you let the sound deeply enter your consciousness. Out of the mouth and in through the ear, around the mind and into the heart, where it waters your soul, as you would water a plant.

3. Gratitude meditation

Gratitude meditation is a practice that will help you remain calm, grounded and appreciative. Gratitude is a fine sentiment, and the alternative – ungratefulness – is universally despised.

For many of us gratitude is an emotion we experience, but for some it's a practice. Gratitude meditation is not a new invention but is deeply rooted in ancient cultures. Monks have for millennia started the day with rituals of gratitude for the blessings of life, thanking the Earth for the food that we eat, the wind for the air that we breathe and our teachers for the wisdom they impart unto us. Also in the West, it was until recently custom to say grace before every meal. Gratitude is universal.

Gratitude meditation is simple. All you need is a peaceful setting for deep contemplation. Find a place where you can be alone with your thoughts, and then think of all the things you are grateful for in life. It can be persons, experiences, opportunities, big and small. It can be something as simple as the air that you breathe, the roof over your head and the miraculous fact that we exist. There is plenty to be thankful for.

In fact, you can enhance the meditation by consciously being thankful not just for the good, but for everything life has to offer. Blessings often come is disguise and if you can learn to see everything as lessons and tests in the school of life, and be thankful for them, then you will always be well-situated despite the dualities of this world, where we inevitably encounter our ups and downs.

GOOD ADVICE

Don't judge your meditation

The mind is a little different every day. Don't get upset or dejected if you for some reason have a hard time focusing on a particular day. Just the attempt itself could be the small thing that will make the difference between a good and a bad day.

The results may not always be perceivable. You may feel that it's not making any difference. But just as children don't notice how they are growing, it can be difficult to see progress from day to day. But if you take a step and see the bigger picture, you will notice huge changes from year to year. They say: "Don't judge each day by the harvest you reap, but by the seeds that you sow."

A tiny effort every day

I have known many, who, with a desire to become better at meditation, attended an intensive course where you are supposed to meditate for ten hours every day. And then they come back feeling like the reincarnation of Buddha, but usually they will not be able to maintain their practice for long. It is much better to establish a good habit that you can continue, than doing something extreme for a short period.

Same time every day

It is recommended you meditate early in the morning. It is a nice way to start the day. If you think "I'll do it later", there is always the risk that something will get in way. The mind is also calmer in the morning, which makes it easier to focus, than in the middle of the day or in the night, after it has been exposed to a myriad of impressions.

If you have become accustomed to meditating at the same time every day, it also makes it easier for the mind to accept that "this is the time we are meditating". The power of habit is mighty. So find out what works for you, and commit to doing it on a daily basis.

Use meditation beads

Meditation or prayer beads are a string with counting beads, which is traditionally used for meditation and prayers in ancient cultures. The way to use it is by fingering one bead as you recite a mantra, take a breath or have a grateful thought before moving your fingers on to the next bead. It is good for concentration, reminds you what you are doing, and gives you a sense of how much time you've spent on your meditation without having to open your eyes and look at the clock or set an alarm.

It is recommended to do a fixed number of rounds on your beads every day. But it should be something that is sustainable. You don't want to end up feeling stressed about having to meditate. You can buy meditations beads at your local temple and yoga studio, or if not, the Internet should do the trick.

Play around with it

You have nothing to lose except stress, anxiety and depression! If you meditate every morning, you can judge the result after a month or so. Full satisfaction or money back guaranteed. If it works wonders for you, that is fantastic! If not, no one is forcing you to continue. I really hope you will give it your best shot. Meditation has changed my life. Who knows, maybe it is just what you need in yours?

SHORT SUMMARY

Meditation is simple and easy

Science now acknowledges the amazing benefits

Experiment, and see what works for you

CHAPTER 16

The early bird catches the worm

"What is night for all living beings is the time of awakening for the self-controlled, and what is the time of awakening for all beings, is night for the introspective sage"
- Bhagavad-Gita

First, I would like to stress, that if you are a night owl, and that works for you – fantastic! Continue, as you like. But for me personally, the transition from sleepyhead to early bird has been so rewarding and helped me in so many ways, that the mere thought of going back seems ridiculous. Why is that? Well the advantages of early rising are numerous and amazing. Here are a few:

A good start

I used to sleep for as long as I could get away with, and sometimes more than that. My parents had to wake me up several times. I would promise them to get up, but feel asleep as soon as they left the room. When I finally pulled myself together, I was late. I had to swallow my breakfast and cut corners to get to school on time. Not a particularly inspiring way to start the day.

Now I jump up as soon as the alarm rings. Keep in mind that is at 2.00 at night. I feel tired, but inspired by the thought of the many leisure hours at my disposal. Moreover, the fatigue usually disappears after a cold shower. If not, I know it's because I need more sleep and then I just compensate with a nap later in the day. Which is easy to afford with a good head start on the day.

The wee hours in the morning are worth gold. I recommend that you use them to make your own home-made morning ritual. Mine, as a monk, consists of prayer, meditation, reading, writing and doing yoga postures. But you know your needs better than I do, and can tailor fit a routine that suits your lifestyle.

The morning hours are my favourite time of day. I rarely sleep in, but if I do, I feel like I've gotten off on the wrong foot, and missed the best part of the day.

Silence

If you sleep in, you are missing one of the most beautiful sights nature has to offer. I love greeting the sun in the morning, sitting on the roof reciting my mantra, as it ascends on the horizon. Thomas Jefferson once said: "The sun has not caught me in bed for 50 years." I look forward to being able to say that myself.

Sunrise

If you sleep in, you are missing one of the most beautiful sights nature has to offer. I love greeting the sun in the morning, sitting on the roof reciting my mantra, as it ascends on the horizon. Thomas Jefferson once said: "The sun has not caught me in bed for 50 years." I look forward to being able to say that myself.

Productivity

The good habit of planning the day in advance, as discussed previously, can be beautifully aligned with a good morning routine. Many share the experience of being far more productive and creative in the morning hours. Whether you are an ambitious competitive person trying to gain the edge, an activist working hard trying save the world, or you just like to get stuff done so you can chill out with a peaceful mind, you can spend the extra time eating a couple of frogs as an appetizer before breakfast.Produktivitet

Den gode vane med at planlægge dagen i forvejen, som vi diskuterede i kapitlet Tænk på papir, harmonerer smukt med en god morgenrutine. Mange deler oplevelsen af at være langt mere produktive og kreative i morgentimerne. Hvis man er et ambitiøst konkurrencemenneske, kan man bruge den ekstra tid på at spise et par frøer inden morgenmad.

Exercise

You can work out whenever you want to of course. I personally prefer doing it early in the morning. First of all, you've just fasted throughout the night, and it's so much better doing yoga and stretches on an empty stomach. Secondly, there is always the risk that something unexpected happens during the day that prevents you from exercising. The only reason to cancel in the morning is sheer laziness.

Breakfast

It is said to be the most important meal of the day. For many that means a cup of coffee nowadays. But if you are an early riser, you have plenty of time to prepare and enjoy and healthy and nutritious breakfast. If you combine it with the 23:1 fast, that is the first and last time you have to think about cooking and eating. What a relief!

If you have roommates, you can also treat them with a delicious morning feast every once in a while. They will love you for it! In the temple where I live, we take turns pampering each other with a first class vegetarian cuisine, made with veggies from our own garden. If you think being a vegetarian is boring and monotonous, you're invited to come and swallow your words along with a delicious meal on the house.

How to become an early riser?

There's the hard way and there's the easy way. The easy way takes some time, but it works nicely. You start by waking up a little earlier than you are used to. Now let that become your new standard. After a while, you tighten the screw and just continue like that till you've reached your ideal.

The hard way is instant. You just jump into it. Set your alarm for way earlier than usual, and rise when it rings. You have to struggle through the day, and stay awake until your new bedtime. Since you've probably been tired all day long, you should fall asleep before the head hits the pillow, and get a good night's sleep. The next day will most likely be easier. Stick to your timings strictly, since a good habit needs time to sink in.

Go to bed earlier

To get to bed in good time is often one of the biggest challenges for the aspiring early bird. If you are used to spend your evenings in front of a screen, it can be difficult to break that pattern. The light from the screen is confusing your brain; tricking it into thinking it is not nearly as late as it really is. Therefore you would do good to leave the screen aside an hour before bedtime, and spend the time gearing down. You can read a good book in your bed, massage yourself and do some relaxed stretching in your pyjamas, meditate for a while or plan tomorrow.

Strategic planning

Is there anything more annoying than an alarm ringing early in the morning? It is way too easy to hit the snooze and fall back into sleep. If you are sceptical about the willpower of tomorrow morning's future you, it is wise to place your alarm strategically at a distance from your bed. This way you'll be forced to get up, once you're up, you just have to stay up.

Strategisk planlægning

Der er få ting, der tester éns selvdisciplin som lyden af et vækkeur tidligt om morgenen. Det er kun alt for nemt at komme til at slå det fra og sove videre. Derfor er det en god ide at placere alarmen i en strategisk god afstand fra sengen, så man er tvunget til at stå op.

What motivates you?

It is early Saturday morning. I tumble out of bed, hurry down the stairs and launch into the couch where I grab the remote control. Why? Cartoons! It is a strong motivation for six year old Jakob not to miss Pokémon on television. I write this to illustrate the point that having something inspiring to wake up to is essential. If you don't have something important to do with your life, then you might as well sleep it away. So rather than asking 'how to wake up early', it may be powerful to ask 'why?' If 'why' is clear, the 'how' will follow.

Use time wisely

Don't wake up early just to watch television for an hour or two, unless you're six years old and they are showing Pokémon again. Time is by far the most precious commodity we have. Benjamin Franklin said this beautifully: "If thou love life, then do not squander time, that is the stuff life is made of." This is one of my favourite quotes related to self-discipline.

Better to use time progressively by getting a good start to the day. Right now, I am sitting here writing. I had a nice long morning meditation, I then enjoyed some peaceful reading and most people are not even awake yet! If you'd like more spare time and not scared of pushing your limits, then you're going to love the next chapter.

SHORT SUMMARY

Create an amazing morning routine

Early morning hours are raw potential

Build the habit of rising early

CHAPTER 17

The polyphasical sleeper

"Dream... But don't sleep too much"
- Ukendt

Everyone you know, including doctors, family and friends will probably think and argue against the next point of discussion. This is an experiment for the bold, adventurous, and the slightly foolhardy you may say. If you go for it, know that you are doing so at your own risk and remember to be careful. Excited? Me too!

A short introduction

Polyphasical is a fancy word. It means more phases. Polyphasical sleep is sleeping less, but over several times. It is distinct from the common monophasical sleep, where one sleeps in one long stretch, most often between seven and nine hours.

There are different polyphasical sleeping patterns, and some are more intense than others. For example there is one where sleep is reduced to only two hours a day. But despite the intensity, they all work on the same principle. The point is to reduce your sleep dramatically, and then compensate with short naps during the day. I will not discuss the more intense patterns, as I don't have a lot of personal experience with them, and therefore cannot recommend them with good conscience. Instead I will share what has worked for me with great enthusiasm. But first, some science.

Sleep, diet and health

To ignore sleep deprivation and run on empty is hazardous. Everyone will agree on that. Pouring extra sugar in your coffee to work throughout the night is also not the best solution, if you want a body that can perform in the long run.

We know how it is if we don't get our sleep. We become shadows of ourselves. Studies show, that a consequence of prolonged sleep deprivation is that you become sick, stupid and ugly. That is a very undesirable combination, which we would like to avoid. So the question is, how much sleep do you actually need for optimal health and well-being?

It is often said that one requires eight hours of sleep every night. But is it really that simple? That is equivalent to saying that you need to eat one kilo of food every day without considering what you eat and how you live. Of course, there are many more influences to consider. Let's look at some of those.

If you work out intensively, then you require more sleep to recover. And if one doesn't exercise, then one's health will gradually dwindle and that will also necessitate more time spent sleeping. As I personally prefer to keep my sleep to a minimum, without compromising my energy levels, I've chosen a mild routine of yoga-exercises that promote good health while not exhausting the body excessively.

Diet is also crucial. What you eat and when you eat will have a big impact on how much sleep you need. If you eat shortly before going to sleep that will compromise the quality of your rest. The body cannot efficiently recover and digest at the same time. We have experience that multi-tasking is bringing down our efficiency a lot. This means that one will require more sleep to feel rested if one eats late in the evening. It has been commonly understood by yogis since the dawn of time that regulating eating habits can minimize the need for sleep.

That struck me when I started eating just one meal a day. I suddenly started waking up several hours before my alarm rang. I realised that combining intermittent fasting with a good sleep pattern was literally saving me a couple of hours each day! I eat my daily meal around 09.00 in the morning, and fast throughout the day, going to bed on an empty stomach. In this way, my meal is fully digested and then the body can focus on sleeping while it rests.

You can do a simple experiment to verify this. Try fasting for at least eight hours before going to sleep, and set your alarm for seven hours. Most likely you will wake up before the alarm rings. Then try eating a big meal the next day prior to sleeping for the same seven hours. The difference is stunning. For me, that is one of the key reasons to doing intermittent fasting. I know that if I eat that second meal it is going to cost me two hours the next day.

Stages of sleep

Not all sleep was created equal. There are different stages of sleep with different purposes. Considering that we will spend a big portion of the rest of our lives sleeping, we would do well to understand what they are and how they work. There is light sleep, deep sleep and dream sleep. Normally, one moves cyclically through the stages from light, deep and dream sleep, and repeat the process throughout the night.

Light sleep is a preliminary phase. Most experts agree that not much happens at this point in terms of getting rest. It is something like waiting in line before boarding the Ferris wheel. It is in the stage of deep sleep where things start to happen. The body relaxes completely. The symptoms are absence of eye movements and muscular activity, and it will be difficult to wake one up. At this stage, the physical body is recharged.

Dream sleep, which generally occurs at end of a cycle, is fascinating. The activity in the brain increases and dreams occur. They do so, even if you don't remember. Dreaming is essential for revitalising the brain. The eyes move behind the lids, while the brain is processing information. Dream sleep is crucial to one's learning and memory: it is quite literally like the fuel on which the brain runs.

Generally, we need an hour of deep sleep and two hours of dream sleep in order to function at an optimal level. Light sleep on the other hand is superfluous. It is more or less a waste of time. So in theory, one could do fine with just three hours of sleep. But one must learn how to get to this point.

Get your moneys worth

A person who has adapted to polyphasical sleep can skip light sleep and enter immediately into dream sleep upon lying down to rest. That is considerably more efficient than normal sleep, where the first 90 minutes are spent warming up with light sleep, before something really starts happening.

In a night, the average monophasical sleeper spends 44% of eight hours in light sleep, 16% in deep sleep and the remaining 38 in rem sleep. The polyphasical sleeper on the other hand, can utilise close to 100% of a 30 minute nap having sweet dreams, wake up shortly after with no use of an alarm and with a feeling of having been resting for hours. If we get our required deep sleep at night, then we just need one or two such naps to compensate the rest.

As mentioned, there are several polyphasical sleep patterns, and some are more intense than others. Leonardo Da Vinci is said to have followed a model where two hours of sleep were divided into six naps of twenty minutes throughout the day. I will not discuss all of them, but I stick to a model that has been working for me without compromising my health.

Four hours a night

This model consists of a four-hour core sleep, and two daily naps of 20-30 minutes. The challenge is to fit the naps into your schedule. The benefit is that you get a solid three additional hours in the day compared to the average person. I have organised my life in such a way that I go to rest at 22.00 in the evening, and rise at 02.00 at night. I used to take my first nap before noon, and the second in the afternoon, but have made some adjustments since I first started this practice. More on that later.

This is how you do

First you need a pattern. Start by deciding when to sleep at night, and when you can take your daily rests. When you've made a plan, and the intelligence has been convinced, then you need to start negotiating with body and mind, and get them to accept the proposal.

It is essential, that you stick within the frame of your four hours a night. Four hours is not enough when half of that is wasted with light sleep. That will force one into a state of sleep deprivation. This lack of sleep is actually the key to a successful transition. Without understanding this point, polyphasical sleep is not going to work for you.

One cannot fall asleep without being tired. That's obvious. The lack of sleep will afford us the opportunity of learning to efficiently fall asleep during our scheduled rests, which in the beginning will be insufficient as long as the body hasn't learned to enter dream sleep instantaneously. But as it is said, necessity is the mother of invention. Hungry for revitalisation, the body will be forced to learn the art of dreaming on demand, and absorb the essential value of a nap. This is where the magic happens!

I was astonished, when I first experienced a successful nap. I felt fresh! A little too fresh perhaps. Suspicion arose. Did I oversleep? No, the alarm didn't even ring yet. I had just been gone for 18 minutes. It felt like hours. It took eight days of adaptation. From there, I quickly caught up with my sleep deficiency, and since then I've been grateful for the extra time it has afforded me.

The transition period

It is different from person to person how long it takes to adjust to polyphasical sleeping. But for most, it takes about two weeks to get into it. So don't try to do this just before your final exams. Better plan it into a vacation or sometime when nothing is expected from you, so you don't end up becoming a zombie.

I did a lot of research before jumping into it. It is good to know what challenges you will have to face, so you're prepared when they come. Many quit before fully adjusting to it, and so never really get to taste the fruit of their endeavour. I used a diary as a crutch, where I had noted what others had experienced from day to day of the transition. So when day four came and it read: "This is the toughest part. Keep pushing. There is light at the end of the tunnel", that helped me a lot. To my great relief, my transition wasn't as hard as the ones I've read about. But I am also a monk and a self-discipline addict, and we're all different.

What to expect?

It is difficult to say something very general about the transition period, as we are all different, and so many varieties of influences are involved. However, it is safe to say, that the first couple of weeks will be tough. You will be tired, grumpy and sluggish. At first, it will be difficult to fall asleep during your scheduled naps, which is frustrating when you're already running on empty. You will have dark circles under your bloodshot eyes, so avoid all kinds of beauty pageants and photo-shoots during the transition. In short, expect one or two weeks where you are a little beside yourself.

The first three to seven days are often the worst. This stage is just about survival. Thereafter it becomes easier, as your body becomes more accustomed. It generally takes two weeks to fully adapt to polyphasical sleep. After ten days, I felt better than ever.

It is very important not to oversleep! Oversleeping will

confuse your body; either causing the transition to fail or prolonging it, and that is highly undesirable. This is true not just for the transition period but also after every time you oversleep, because you will have to readjust.

I am still following this pattern, and I intend to stick with it. It has become natural, and I am energetic throughout the day, except once a day I feel my brain starting to slow down, and then I know it is time for my nap. Most days, I just rest once, and sometimes I even forget about it because I am just not tired. But it differs, and there are also days when I need two and even three naps. I listen to my body, and if it's tired, it gets a nap. But I keep it short, so it doesn't get spoiled.

A good investment

The time spent becoming a polyphasical sleeper comes back with a compound interest. The three additional hours every day accumulates to 21 a week. That is 1,092 extra hours every year emerging out of thin air. What would you spend that extra time on?

Famous polyphasical sleepers

There are many great thinkers, artists and saints who used polyphasical sleep patterns to minimise their sleep and maximise their impact on the world. Their lives are testimony to the fact that a reduction of sleep doesn't necessarily reduce intelligence, creativity or compromise our existence, as is often the claim of modern sleep experts.

Nikola Tesla is considered one of histories greatest inventors. Tesla regarded sleep as a complete waste of his time and managed to condense his sleep to two hours a day. We can thank him for alternating currents and many great inventions.

When Napoleon Bonaparte was ruling France, he would reportedly sleep two hours every night and consistently take a nap during the afternoon, even on the battlefield. When he later lost power and was imprisoned, his spirit went down and he became a sleepyhead.

When Leonardo Da Vinci was not busy painting the Mona Lisa, invent weaponry or design the first air planes, he would take a nap every now and then. Allegedly, he slept ten minutes every other hour throughout the day.

Srila Prabhupada, the greatest proponent of Indian philosophy in the modern age, would rest an hour after breakfast, an hour after lunch and at night, he would sleep somewhere between one and three hours. He minimised his sleep, so he would have time to translate and comment on the ancients Vedas, the scriptures of India, and make them available for the English-speaking world.

Thomas Edison, Salvador Dali and many others deserve to be on the list, but trying to keep a little book little, they will unjustly be left out. Sorry.

Additional benefits

The extra hours are the polyphasical sleeper's greatest gain, but there are a few smaller prizes that are worth mentioning too.

1) Say goodbye to sleepless nights. With polyphasical sleeping it has never been easier falling asleep. I feel the drowsiness announcing itself twenty minutes before bedtime, and sleep

soundly within seconds of having lied down. Works every time.

2) What is more annoying than waking up in the dead of night having to pee? Polyphasical sleep solves that, since it is much easier to retain your water for four hours than eight.

Conclusion

Polyphasical sleeping works on the principle of quality over quantity. Yes, you sleep less. But you sleep better and more efficiently, and from my experience I can say that if it is practiced properly there is no harm.

SHORT SUMMARY

Learn to skip the stage of light sleep

Diet and exercise effect the need for sleep

Gain three hours daily by polyphasical sleep

3. PART

MOTIVE

"If one advances confidently in the direction of his dreams, and endeavours to live the life which he has imagined, he will meet with a success unexpected in common hours." - Henry David Thoreau - American writer

The third and last point of the book is about motive. The Sanskrit word prayojana means "the ultimate necessity". That is the goal and what inspires us to act.

I have previously used the example that the shortest distance between two points is a straight line. Prayojana is the second point in our equation. So when the required knowledge is obtained, as per the first point, and one has defined a worthy goal – what one wants from life – then you can build a bridge between the two, using the tools and habits from the second part.

Where the second part was more methodical, this part is more philosophical, for when one is figuring out, what one wants from life, a relevant question is: "Why?" We have so many desires and ambitions, but what is the reason behind them? What is it we expect to find at the end of the rainbow, and is it even to be found where we are looking?

CHAPTER 18

Why?

"Before you start some work, always ask yourself three questions - Why am I doing it, What the results might be and Will I be successful. Only when you think deeply and find satisfactory answers to these questions, go ahead." "
- Canakya Pandit

Why do we do, what we do?

I once had some guests visiting the temple who were filming a television show,. They were curious and asked a lot of questions. "Why do you rise so early?" "Why do you live in celibacy?" "Why are you vegetarian?" While patiently answering them, the camera man suddenly exclaimed: "If you were to ask me, why I do what I do, I would have no idea what to say!"

As children, we ask questions from morning to evening, but growing up we often become so used to our patterns, that we forget to question them. That should never happen! So many people live and die without ever asking why, drinking the ritualistic morning coffee before going to school or work, spending the day at the office, watching television in the evening and looking forward to the weekend. Why? We live our lives, knowing what we do, and how to do it, but we often forget about the 'why'.

The Vedas define the primary characteristic of a human being as our ability to ask questions. What is it we expect to achieve going through the motions of life? If you know why you are looking, what you are looking and how to find it, you can better estimate if you are moving in the right direction. If not, then start with why. If the first figure in the calculation is wrong, it will invalidate the whole thing and the result will be off.

Say you know what you want, and you have some idea about how to achieve it. But then the question is "will you be satisfied if you find it?", there is a tendency to believe that the grass is greener on the other side, and that happiness is waiting around the corner. That with a few adjustments, life will fall perfectly into place. But how can we be so sure?

Cards on the table

Let me be straightforward with you. My claim is that the sooner you can realise your dreams, the sooner you will realise that is not where happiness is to be found.

Many believe that money will solve their problems, that success is the highest attainment, that a beautiful lover will fill the void in their hearts. But is that the case? What do we ultimately find in these desirables? Not that they are empty and meaningless, but that they are not enough, insufficient in quenching our thirst. The grass remains greener on the other side.

Who am I to talk about money, success or love? I am just a kid who became a monk. It may have more impact coming from the famous actor Jim Carrey: "I think everybody should get rich and famous and do everything they ever dreamed of so they can see that it's not the answer."

It can be frustrating to pursue and realise the dream, only

to discover that it is not enough. We sometimes see ridiculously successful people ending up taking their own lives, and still so many want to follow in their footsteps, seeking happiness in the externals. If that is what they want, they should have it, so that they will see, it is not the answer.

It is my conviction, and an echo of the Vedic conclusions that material success disconnected with a higher purpose can never satisfy the soul, but the experience of frustration in fulfilment of ambition may initiate a search for higher purpose and values in life. That is why I wrote this book. To fast-forward the progressive march toward material success and subsequent frustration. I am not trying to force my philosophy down your throat, but I hope you'll find it between the lines.

A celibate monk with a hidden agenda

You may have heard of the Kama Sutra. It is an ancient Indian text, relating secrets of heavenly sex, helping the readers satisfy their sexual appetite. It was written more than 2,000 years ago, and has been extremely popular all over the world and still is to this day.

What's interesting is that the author of Kama Sutra, Vatsyayana, wrote the book while living in celibacy. He understood that people in general had to outlive their lusty desires beyond the point of saturation. With the Kama Sutra, he supplied a helping hand to accelerate the process. Why? Because one cannot speak philosophy to a hungry man.

SHORT SUMMARY

Whatever you do, never stop asking 'why?'

Dreams may come true, but will we be happy?

Success without higher purpose is empty

CHAPTER 19

The value of life

"The ultimate value of life depends upon awareness and the power of contemplation rather than upon mere survival."
- Aristotle

Dangerous self-discipline

Self-discipline is freedom, a potential that can be misused. When scientists were working on the first nuclear bombs, surely they must have mustered a lot of self-discipline. So much destruction and evil has been brought about by self-disciplined individuals with bad intentions and distorted values. As such, self-discipline in the wrong hands is like a monkey with a hand grenade.

Self-discipline is freedom, and with freedom comes responsibility. Therefore it is important, that we are in contact with the better part of our deepest values, having a strong positive purpose guiding our actions. I believe we were all created with admirable values, but that they can easily become covered by negative influences in a crazy world.

You are probably not the next Adolf Hitler or Joseph Stalin, but it would be very unusual if you were not also influenced by greed, envy and hatred. Such defects of character are in Sanskrit called anartha, which means 'unwanted' or 'worthless'. It is considered so, because it hinders our experience of the genuine satisfaction that arises when we exist in harmony with our true nature and identity.

It is a fact that the modern world is full of distorted values; especially the media is guilty of glamorising stupid role models and romanticising superficial success. Of course that affects us, and therefore we may have a hard time discriminating between that is actually valuable to us, and what is not.

What gives value to your life?

Many of our values are dormant in our subconsciousness, but through an introspective soul-searching experiment, you can bring out these fundamental core values, that you will bring a greater sense of purpose and fulfilment to your life. If you do it wholeheartedly, I guarantee a tremendous learning experience.

Imagine you are at a funeral. You observe the sadness in the grief-stricken faces of friends and family. The whole room is pulsating with emotions. You sense both the joy of having known and the sorrow of having lost.

You know all the guests. After all, it is your funeral. They have come to say goodbye. Who showed up? What would you hope, that they would remember you for? What would they say about you, and what would you wish they'd say about you? If you reflect on this deeply, you should be left with a clear understanding of what matters to you the most, and an increased awareness of your true values.

You can go deeper by inviting a guest of honour, a fly on the wall that has seen it all. A person who can see right through you, knowing you better than you know yourself.

A witness, or God personified for that matter. What is He thinking of you? Is He looking upon your life with pride or disappointment? If you can look Him in the eyes unashamed, it is a sign that you've lived a life of integrity in harmony with your true values. If not, maybe it's about time to change some things? Imagine if He is real!

Put your life in perspective

We all have to die at some point. Many find this to be an inconvenient truth, and prefer to ignore it. As a child, I would often lay awake late at night thinking of death. It was simultaneously fascinating and scary. Mostly scary. But it is healthy to contemplate death. It puts life in perspective.

To live every day as it would be your last is just not practical, for if you want to accomplish something with your life, it's going to take more than a day. But remind yourself of death often, and that it may come unexpectedly. That will insure you don't squander life with unimportant trivialities that you will later regret.

Die with good conscience

After a good day's work comes a good night's sleep. You could compare it with a person who has dedicated his life to doing good, so he can leave this world with good conscience. For me, that means living my life as a service to my fellow human beings and other living entities. As a service more than a burden to Mother Earth, and in the ultimate sense for the pleasure of God who I like to call Krishna.

No matter where I look I see the universe. I guess that means I'm the middle of it all, right? That is the egocentric conception of life. If we think that this world is here for our satisfaction, we are living in an illusion. This narrow-minded outlook on life is good for nothing. It will only bring about troubles, so we should rise above it.

The point is living life so you can die with good conscience. What that means may be individual, but wouldn't it be amazing to look back at a life you could be genuinely proud of, without no regrets and nothing to feel ashamed of. And then to die with peace of mind, knowing you gave it your best shot, not scared but excited, wondering what is going to happen on the other side?

SHORT SUMMARY

Self-discipline should be the servant of purpose

Understand your values and live by them

Live a life you can look back on without shame

CHAPTER 20

Don't waste time

"Dost thou love life? Then do not squander time, for that is the stuff life is made of." "
- Benjamin Franklin

Time is mysterious. We can try to understand it but it is beyond our comprehension. It was here before us, and will remain after we're gone. It controls the life of every atom, star and galaxy. Everyone is under its jurisdiction. It doesn't pay attention to whether you are rich or poor, young or old, knowledgeable or have the IQ of an avocado.

Its influence is everywhere. Still, we cannot quite put our finger on it. Cannot quite figure it out. It is a puzzle that the brightest minds in human history have tried to solve. The Bhagavad-gita, however, has an interesting perspective.

Krishna tells Arjuna about a universal form, the impersonal aspect of the absolute. Arjuna curiously inquires from Krishna, if He can show it to him. Krishna then reveals to Arjuna the sum total of the universe, complete with past, present and future, all in one place.

Arjuna becomes overwhelmed. He doesn't know what to with himself. His personal existence all of a sudden seems completely insignificant, reduced to a flash in the eternity of time. He witnesses time's parallel forces of creation and destruction. He sees how everything emerges for a moment, only to rush towards inevitable annihilation in the jaws of time.

Terrified Arjuna asks: "Who are you?" The answer is unmistakably clear: "I am Time, the destroyer of worlds." Sometimes we speak about killing time, but that is not going to happen. It is the other way around. Time is killing us!

For every second we are closer to death. A single moment cannot be bought back for all the wealth in the world. They say time is money. But isn't that little foolish? You can spend time earning money, but you can never reverse the process, so time always wins over money. What then could be a great loss or squandering of valuable resources? What catastrophe is equivalent to wasting time? For wasting one's time is wasting one's life.

We have 86.400 seconds at our disposal every day. What do we use them on? How much time is simply slipping through our hands, without our catching hold of it and doing something worthwhile with it? It would be an awful shame one day to look back at one's life with an uncomfortable dissatisfaction at heart and think: "Was that really it? Was that all I managed to do? It went too fast! Where did the time go?"

I am not entitled to tell you, what you should do with your life, despite wanting to do so. That is not my right. We have all been granted free will, which contributes to making life beautiful, variegated and unpredictable. I have tried to give you the essence of what I have learned about self-discipline on my journey. You are free to use this information as you like, but I hope, that you will use it to live a life that is worthy of a child of Krishna, and that will bring about a satisfied smile to His face.

SHORT SUMMARY

Time is the building block of life

Time is the most valuable resource

Try making Krishna smile